THE MOTHER TREE

Discovering the Love and Wisdom of Our Divine Mother

Kathryn Knight Sonntag

Paperback: 978-1-953677-11-2
eBook: 978-1-953677-12-9
Audiobook: 978-1-953677-13-6

Library of Congress Control Number: 2020948308

Printed in the United States of America.

Faith Matters Publishing
2929 W Navigator Drive, Suite 400
Meridian, ID 83642

faithmatters.org

For Kristine

Acknowledgments

So many conversations with fellow seekers made this book possible. I'm indebted to a host of women writers, scholars, storytellers, and prophetesses who have opened the way to the Divine Feminine. These women, including Margaret Barker, Carol Lynn Pearson, and Maxine Hanks, are spiritual guides for whom I am eternally grateful. Thank you to Elizabeth Pinborough and Katherine Indermaur for their keen editorial eyes. Thank you to George Handley, Kristine Haglund, Dayna Patterson, and Morinda Cottam for their excellent suggestions. Thank you to Bill Turnbull and Faith Matters Foundation for entrusting this project to me; I am deeply honored. Thank you, always, to Bob Sonntag, who made countless extra meals and changed countless extra diapers so I could write. And thank you, finally, to Amber Richardson, for the multiple close reads, the grace and love with which you attended to this work.

Contents

PREFACE

Why Seek the Mother Tree?

As Latter-day Saints, we believe that "our theology begins with heavenly parents,"[1] and yet there is a conspicuous silence surrounding what it means for us to have a Divine Mother individually and collectively. The reality of a Heavenly Mother in our doctrine is explicit. A recent work, "'A Mother There': A Survey of Historical Teachings about Mother in Heaven," documents a substantial number of references to Her reality and nature, comprising "over six hundred sources of all types referencing a Heavenly Mother in Mormon and academic discourse since 1844."[2] Statements about the Mother from Church leaders affirm Her as heavenly wife and parent, co-creator with the Father, co-framer of the plan of salvation, an involved parent during our mortality, and our Mother after we leave this earthly realm.[3] These identities alone give me reason to seek Her and to understand more fully Her role in my salvation and the salvation of the world.

While I always believed in Heavenly Mother, it was when I began to desire to know Her that I felt Her absence most keenly: from the plan of salvation, our temples, and our weekly Sunday meetings. I felt Her absence in our worship and our conceptions of spiritual parentage. I began to understand the Divine Feminine as an integral source of my divine essence, real to me since childhood; and while my Heavenly Queen was so unshakably a part of my soul, She was missing from institutionalized representations of God. I continue to ask: What parts of me come from my Mother? What is She like? What wisdom and love are uniquely Hers to give, and how does She teach and guide me in mortality? Is She merely nodding alongside the Father as He gives counsel and commands, or does She have something uniquely Hers to impart?

More and more of Her children are sensing an existential need to know Her. I don't know all of the answers—none of us do—but that doesn't mean there are no answers or firm conclusions that we can draw. I believe asking questions and exploring possibilities are indispensable ways to show love and reverence for revealed truth.

My desire to better understand old and new dimensions of my female experience is inseparable from my desire to know Her. The fruit of my initial inquiries materialized as a collection of poetry called *The Tree at the Center*, which explores the Mother as She appears in my experiences as a new mother, in world cultures (symbolized as the tree of life), and in the natural world. As a poet, I find great satisfaction and enlightenment in exploring metaphors. Their power to convey vivid imagery that transcends literal meanings ignites the imagination, inviting active participation in what can result in sacred sensorial experiences, spiritual revelation, and new intellectual considerations. In *The Mother Tree*, I offer the same ancient metaphor that helps me contemplate Heavenly Mother. I offer my thoughts about the tree in reverence with the hope that it helps to keep the doctrine of our Mother from neglect. With this book, I wish to provide room for all seekers to explore, where we can consider together who the Mother is, why She has been seemingly absent, and how we can approach Her through the image of the tree that holds Her in profound framing.

We are accustomed to expressing in concrete words that God the Father and Jesus are individual beings with knowable attributes. The way is not made to know Heavenly Mother equally; She resides in shadow. This creates a theological understanding of God the Mother that is potentially more mysterious and different from the theological landscape of God the Father and Jesus. It is new territory. Although Jesus is a specific being, we also come to know Him through metaphor: as the Lamb, the Bread of Life, the Way. We can discuss God the Mother through symbolic language because She is cloaked in the metaphor of the tree throughout the scriptures. Mother takes us even further into a symbolic realm where divine femininity is able to make itself known as generative, intuitive, compassionate, a complement to divine masculinity. Further exploration of the Mother is part of the unfolding Restoration in our hearts. It is needed now more than ever.

As children of heavenly parents, we embody traits from each parent. Because we have come to understand God as He, the majority of our discussion about divine attributes we seek to emulate originate from a male deity. We have had little experience thinking of God as feminine and masculine, let alone considering Mother God as an autonomous, whole being with unique traits that we, as Her spirit children, have also inherited. We are less experienced at seeking out the Mother's attributes. I believe that a knowledge of Her character, power, and purpose creates wholeness in ourselves, in our relationships, and in our theology. Harmonizing Their divinely feminine and divinely masculine principles inside our souls leads to unity with Them. For this work of harmonizing, we can come to the Mother Tree.

NOTES

1 Dallin H. Oaks, "Apostasy and Restoration," *Ensign*, May 1995, 84. Elder Oaks taught this principle in general conference: "Our theology begins with heavenly parents. Our highest aspiration is to be like them."

2 David L. Paulsen and Martin Pulido, "'A Mother There': A Survey of Historical Teachings about Mother in Heaven," *BYU Studies Quarterly* 50, no. 1 (2011): 76.

3 Paulsen and Pulido, "'A Mother There,'" 80–84.

Introduction

The tree of life has always called to me. When I was a child, I would read Lehi's vision in the Book of Mormon and feel drawn in by its ecstatic presence. I sensed there was more to the symbol than I could then grasp. Over the years, I found a thread of groves and trees running through ancient and modern revelatory experiences, though I was unsure of the significance. I reencountered the symbol of the tree of life as I prepared my master's thesis on the role of the transcendent in landscapes. I engaged more intimately with the sacred symbol as I learned about its archetypal power. I finally grasped what my childhood self was sensing: the tree implores my soul to reveal its truest self.

One resonance that struck me most was the tree as an image of eternal life inextricably linked to the Divine Feminine. It felt like no coincidence that I became pregnant with my first child as the tree's power to invoke sacred connections between the earth and the heavens was unfolding in my consciousness. I felt the tree return and re-center inside my soul, filling an absence I had sensed my whole life but could never fully articulate. As my first child grew inside me, the revelation that I was a tree of life distilled upon[1] me: like the tree of life, I connected heaven and earth as I brought a soul into the world. The symbolism of the tree lived in my very limbs and heart.

Inseparable from my new understanding of the tree of life was the revelation of a Mother God in scripture. I found Her first in the book of Proverbs, named there as Wisdom, the tree of life.[2] The eternal presence of the Mother, rooted in my own religious heritage, continued to be unveiled, and I saw Her everywhere: in the Garden of Eden, the Garden of Gethsemane, the Sacred Grove, Lehi's tree of life, the first temple in Jerusalem, Abraham's sacred Oak of Moreh, and the cross from which Jesus's body hung. Her presence beckoned me to make more profound connections to my own divinity. I discovered, in the image of the tree, a reflection of my yearnings for unity with the divine, with wisdom, wholeness, and renewal. I experienced, once again, how our scriptures become alive and bright, responsive and renewed, by our engagement with them.[3]

Join me on a journey through the three primary zones, or realms, of the tree—roots, trunk, crown—that represent three different regions of our spiritual journey, as a way to discover our Divine Mother in each place. As we consider the botanical and symbolic expressions of the tree, we are able, by the final pages of the book, to hold a more integral vision of our Mother, one that weaves together Her tender maternity and Her exquisite power to bind together in love.

As with all things sacred, I have found the Divine Feminine to be beyond the structure and confines of language. We find Her substance, Her language, Her voice, Her abundance in symbolic expressions, layered and transmuting, ever evolving as we develop our discerning of both what is knowable and the godliness beyond mortal comprehension. While no language can adequately describe the holy, I hope this journey toward the very real presence of the Divine Feminine can aid our understanding of how She manifests on our path toward becoming.

While I have devoted some scholarship and years of study to this topic, the knowledge I hold most sacred comes from personal experience with God, Mother and Father. Any wisdom I have to share on this subject grows from earnest seed-questions in my heart that continue to be nurtured by divine love. I extend the pattern of this quest to you and invite you to bring your own discernment and desires for healing and truth to these pages as you read. In fact, your active participation is essential. As you continue to experience the Mother, to grow in Her nature and nurture, I hope that the transcendent power of Her love enlivens you to expand your soul's engagement with faith, love, and peace.

NOTES

1 Doctrine and Covenants 121:45.

2 Proverbs 3:18.

3 Alma 37:3–5. I love Alma's description of the enlivening power of holy texts: "And now behold, if they are kept they must retain their brightness."

The Mother Tree

From the Bible and the Book of Mormon, we are familiar with the tree as a salvific image. Most familiar to us is the tree of life envisioned by both Lehi and Nephi, symbolizing the love of God and eternal life. Perhaps less familiar is the depiction found in Jacob 5. The allegory of Zenos, quoted by Jacob, reveals one of the most beautiful and grace-filled portrayals of a tree as a maternal figure gathering souls for salvation. In three different verses, the tame tree is called the mother tree.[1] She nourishes and grows her natural and grafted branches with the help of the servant and the Lord of the vineyard, providing life for all who will accept her redemptive powers. The tree image connects maternal care to the saving powers of God, our divine parents.

Together we will explore this simple and profound connection between the maternal and the salvific, united in the symbol of the tree. Engaging with an expansive framing of our Mother's selfhood, wisdom, power, and love, we will find in Her an essential guide on our personal journeys of transformation. We will learn, through both the materiality and spirituality of our Mother God, Her portion of care for our journeys of transformation and how She, as the tree, frames the journey itself. Wisdom about Her becomes wisdom from Her; in knowing Her, we are changed into truer versions of ourselves with eyes more able to see that She has been with us all along. Recognizing Her place in our faith journeys, and consequently in our Latter-day Saint theology, reflects the order of the heavens and restores a vision of wholeness and healing that our hearts desperately seek.

As mentioned in the introduction, each portion of the tree reveals characteristics of our Divine Mother. In the diagram that follows, we see the tree and its three distinct parts—roots, trunk, crown—corresponding to three different regions—underworld, earth, heavens. As Latter-day Saints, we are very comfortable with the idea of Earth as the place of our mortal existence and with the heavens above symbolizing the life to come, but the idea of an underworld is less familiar. For now, we will simply say that it is an internal region that we experience on Earth, a place of beliefs, introspection, ancestral wisdom, and spiritual rebirth.

NOTES

1 Jacob 5:54, 56, 60.

THE COSMIC TREE

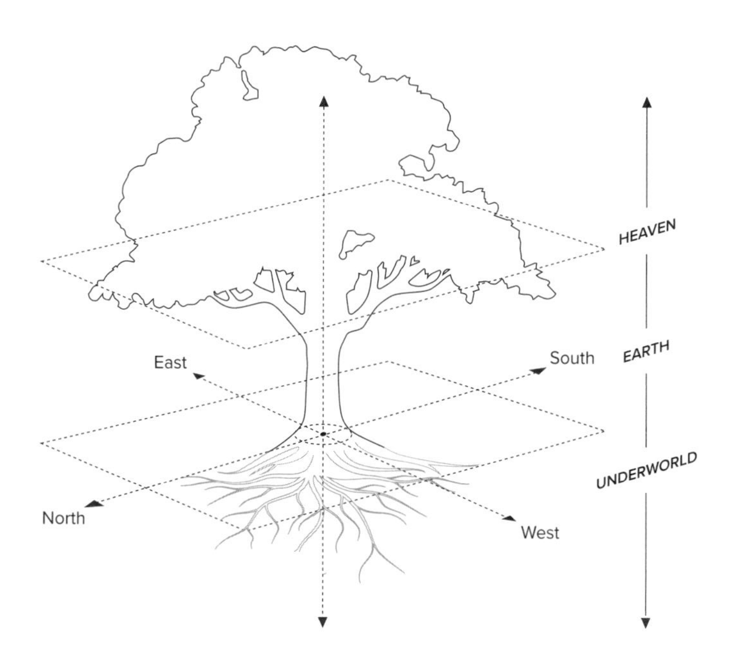

Diagram of the Cosmic Tree. As we familiarize ourselves with this diagram, we can begin to play with symbolic layering, to see the roots as the past, the trunk as the present, and the branches as the future, for example. The symbol of the tree can also manifest three ways of knowing: the intuition of the shadowlands, the experiential knowledge of the earth, and the imaginal wisdom of the heavens.

CHAPTER ONE

Roots

Underworld: Below All Things

The underworld, as seen in our diagram, is the region of the roots. We begin our journey descending into this place where life begins, into the underground where roots break free from seed and become the most permanent and stabilizing part of the tree.[1] Roots withstand severe climatic conditions, storing sometimes millennia of experience.[2] Incredibly, we are discovering that root tips function like brains, passing electric currents and storing important information.[3]

Root systems take in water and nourishment in order to grow the tree, but they do nothing alone. Recent scientific research has opened our minds to the intricate workings of forest ecologies and the ways in which trees respond, communicate, and care for each other. Whole networks of organisms speak to each other, sending chemical signals below the ground. Roots call to fungi, to the root systems of surrounding trees, exchanging nourishment, information, and energy.

Just as intact root tips register changes—such as toxic substances, stones, and changes in soil—when roots are pruned, the "brain-like structures are cut off along with the sensitive tips."[4] This causes disorientation for the roots and interferes with the tree's ability to sense direction underground.[5] Its roots begin to grow only very shallowly, which keeps the tree from accessing needed water and nutrients.

We are discovering how the elder trees of the forest, the mother trees (the biggest, oldest trees with the most fungal connections, not necessarily females), are the keepers of wisdom. "When Mother Trees—the majestic hubs at the center of forest communication, protection, and sentience—die, they pass their wisdom to their kin, generation after generation, sharing the knowledge of what helps and what harms, who is friend or foe, and how to adapt and survive in an ever-changing landscape."[6] The older trees in the forest discern which neighboring saplings are their own kin. Mother trees connect with their young, conspecifics, and many surrounding species through their root systems, passing sugars and other nutrients.[7]

In the gnarl of beetles and rot, in the communion of roots and fungi, we find powerful life forces, creatures who remind us of the ways in which death is woven into life in endless cycles. The work of the roots speaks to the hidden mysteries that unfold in the dark. They remind us that the dark is alive.

The underground plane symbolizes a place of spiritual growth and regeneration, of knowledge creation. Here, in this womb space, the unseen and obscured portions of both tree and soul reside. As we know from Alma 32 in the Book of Mormon, we must plant good seeds in good soil to expect our soul-tree to thrive and expand into eternal life. Here we are asked to evaluate the soil and how it has affected our roots. What beliefs, traditions of our fathers (from our literal ancestry and our cultural inheritance), and experiences may be keeping us from our full potential? What needs to be uprooted?

I like to think of the realm of the roots as the holding space for introspection and reevaluation of our true identities. A comprehension of this repository of hard-won wisdom and sustenance is necessary for our growth. As such, it demands everything from us, our full presence of mind, body, spirit, and heart. The darkness we encounter here asks us in quiet and measured ways to sit with it, to allow its slow workings to speak to the hidden, ineffable parts of us.

Many of us are afraid of the dark, but even more of us are afraid of being afraid. Mother God teaches us how to let our eyes adjust to the dim, and that the discomfort inherent in this common experience of the unknown encourages us to tend to our fears. So often, the darkness (the unknown, the unfamiliar, the unpleasant, the painful) is "the very next place where God is preparing to build [our] trust."[8] While fear exposes the limits of our present capacity, it also can be the perfect tool to reveal our potential capacity. During their own descent into the depths of Liberty Jail, Joseph Smith and his companions reflected on the necessity of soul-transforming experience, including a deep exploration of the shadows, as a prerequisite to leading another soul to the same path of radical growth: "Thy mind . . . if thou would lead a soul unto salvation, must stretch as high as the utmost Heavens, and search into and contemplate the lowest considerations of the darkest abyss, and expand upon the broad considerations of eternal expanse. Thou must commune with God."[9] We do this work not only for our own growth but also to prepare us to help others move toward transformation. Perhaps most poignantly, I have found that the feminine realm of the roots teaches us to face what we don't understand, not with fear, hatred, or resentment but with acceptance, with the open heart of presence. It asks for a commitment to reinvention as we stare into the face of what is unresolved inside us.

This place of initiation can be extremely uncomfortable because of its uncertainties, unexpected pains, and the ways in which it will challenge some deeply held beliefs. The divinely feminine aspect of each of us calls for our perception of and devoted attention to the finer feelings, energies, and expressions of spirit woven throughout the living world, beckoning our souls to transgress beyond the edge of what we know so we may grow and create good fruit. It requires us to develop sovereignty—greater self-governing power and authority—before it allows us to progress on our spiritual journeys. We find the Mother waiting for us in this place of descent so that we may discover ourselves, and in doing so, begin to discover Her.

My life has taught me that deep feeling blooms deep knowing. And deep feeling requires deep listening. During my early teen years, I spent many hours sitting beneath my bedroom window watching the sky. The ceiling of my upstairs room sloped to a bench seat below a large skylight. As I sat, I could see out to the north face of Mount Olympus. I was particularly drawn to sit and watch on stormy days, during sunsets, at dusk, or under the slanting light of spring and autumn—times when the sky spoke of change.

I was most aware of my own internal state at these times and felt my soul's need to create. Some days I would read or write poetry as I watched. Others, I would listen to hours of music. I knew on some level that I needed that time to reconcile and weave together the reality of my life—its pain and disappointments as well as its joy—with the larger visions I had for myself and the world. My room became a sanctuary because I found myself there. The self that was revealed was a self deeply loved by God and deeply known. This direct connection to the divine oriented me during the most excruciating times of my life.

We believe that Jesus's descent below all things, into pain and suffering, allowed Him to ascend above all things on His path to becoming our Savior. Like Jesus, we are called to descend into the shadows of our own souls, to face our internal wounds and unfinished parts so that we may also transform and expand toward greater light on our journeys of becoming. On the threshold of our journey, I would ask you to consider the context of the two great descents of Jesus on Earth—His earthly battlegrounds, if you will. The places that held Jesus through His atoning were the garden and the cross, an olive grove and a felled tree. Could it be that the Mother Tree was His support in His greatest need? What could this teach us about our own descents?

The Descent

> *The Creation Mother is always also the Death Mother and vice versa. Because of this dual nature, or double-tasking, the*

great work before us is to learn to understand what around and about us and what within us must live, and what must die.[10]

—Clarissa Pinkola Estés

As I turn inward, Mother asks me to question what matters. What if the cultural identifiers of merit by which I have perceived my worth were taken away, stripped from me as they were from Job? What of me remains? I attempt to see what is real, to follow the path of my heavenly parents and brother to do the work of reckoning and let die in me the things I think I ought to uproot in others.[11] I try to tune into the emotional and intuitive landscapes of my soul and the more nuanced ways of relating to the world.

A profound inward listening allows for what is to be. Many times this looks like turning inward to face, admit to, and acknowledge pain. Tuning into our own pain (which so often includes the sorrow we feel watching those we love suffer), we allow it to fully express itself so that our hearts can experience it completely. In this state of vulnerability, our suffering is sanctified. Connections are made. Our chemical makeup alters, imprinted with expansive emotional landscapes. As poet Rainer Maria Rilke so beautifully described, in facing our shadow sides, we experience our "grief cries" as the mercy that defines our God and that allows us to be found in the abyss:

It's possible I am pushing through solid rock
in flintlike layers, as the ore lies, alone;
I am such a long way in I see no way through,
and no space: everything is close to my face,
and everything close to my face is stone.

I don't have much knowledge yet in grief
so this massive darkness makes me small.
You be the master: make yourself fierce, break in:
then your great transforming will happen to me,
and my great grief cry will happen to you.[12]

Christ's suffering in the Garden of Gethsemane created a deep and resounding connection to divinity as well as to us. Our suffering can also connect us to each other and to our heavenly parents. Mother God holds us, as She did Her son Jesus, in the extremity of pain.

In the greatest paradox of mortal life, it is human nature to fear the most divine part of ourselves: our ability to heal, and in so doing, to metaphorically gain new life through new eyes. To grow in seership. Many times we wish instead, perhaps subconsciously, to turn to our own ignorance,[13] to suppress that which represents growth because it is the unknown. Because it will ask hard things of us and cause pain. Many times, this lack of demonstrated faith—this unwillingness to progress on our path of discipleship through healing—speaks to our perhaps unacknowledged resentment of the fundamental purpose of life, which is to change. We hold firm to our mindsets and to our known paradigms under the illusion of control. Little do we recognize, at first, that what we are ultimately saying is that at-one-ment is not something we really desire, that we prefer our comfortable gods, made in our own image. Our Mother, here in the dark, asks us to let go, to awaken and rouse our faculties. To feel all there is to feel.

I have felt the presence of the Mother in some of my most difficult descents. In the first trimester of my second pregnancy,

I miscarried. A close friend came to offer comfort, and I found myself unable to speak about what had happened. I had no words. After she left, all I wanted was to be flat on my back on the earth. I laid down under the crab apple tree in my front yard. I felt my breathing slow and my body relax. I attended only to the presence of the tree: its undulating branches, red fruit, and peeling bark. As I held the moment in my soft gaze, the energy of its living form filled my knowing, and somehow I was found by the tree. I felt it aware of my presence, and in that mutual acknowledgment, a communion of some significant way. I was embraced in the tree's knowing that everything *was*, and that was enough.

I saw my Mother in the tree, Her power to connect living souls above in the heavens to the mortal realm below, and in the tree's composite of life and death. The upper canopy of this old crab apple comprised a gnarl of brittle black branches, a clear sign that the tree was dying. Yet its skirting branches were producing perhaps a double offering of fruit in what seemed to be an effort to make up for what the dead branches could no longer offer. This tree was giving everything to rebirth while surrendering to a slow decline. It embodied the endless cycle of life-death-life I had come to associate with the Mother and the same divine creative powers in me. The manifestation of God before me in the form of that tree was showing me how to be in the pain to find pain's cure.

I felt raw about my struggles with my earthly mother as I grieved. While she did her best and cared for me in many ways, basic needs were left unmet during my childhood. As an adult, I carried the melancholy of emotional distance; I realized I felt largely unmothered. Though I didn't have the words to articulate my feelings at first, I soon understood that I carried a mother wound, one that enhanced my longing for a wise woman, a sage who could point me down the path of the feminine way and hold space for all I was and all I carried on the journey.

My experiences and study led me to see that we have a Mother wound in our theology. This theological phenomenon is a collective wound that has affected our ability to perceive the need for the Mother as individuals. The spiritual death we experience in mortality, the fall into this telestial state, includes not only a separation from God the Father but also a separation from God the Mother. Just as unexamined pain—be it feelings of unworthiness, abandonment, or anger—can keep us from a clear perspective on what is happening inside and outside of us, our unacknowledged wound caused by separation from our spiritual Mother likewise obscures our vision of ourselves and the divine. The ramifications of what it means to be separated from our Mother are yet to be fully uncovered and understood.

None of us comes close to a complete understanding of who our heavenly parents are in this life, yet having an obscured or limited view of who we are doesn't mean that They aren't available to us. On the contrary. I have found that it is in the recognition of the distance and the desire to close the gap that we are tenderly cared for. The goal is to remove as much of the distortions and noise around our true essence and beauty, and thus Theirs, as we can. Simply put, I believe that what Joseph Smith said—those who do not comprehend the character of God do not comprehend themselves—applies to both the

Mother and the Father.[14] And so I wonder, How is it possible to know ourselves wholly if we do not know the Mother?

Stepping into the dark unknown creates space in our hearts for greater comprehension of the eternal interplay between light and shadow. Our very presence here in the realm of the roots conveys our willingness to dive down deep, to progress on individualized yet profoundly interconnected paths toward the divine. As Jesus did, we face our shadows and the forces that would divide us to find greater light. We experience pain as a part of the path to becoming and move through it in order to shed old ways that no longer serve us. We begin to sense that the degree to which we feel and acknowledge our soul's discord is the degree to which we can fully embody the joy of progression. Fear and faith. Light and dark. Feminine and masculine. These are not ultimately opposing forces but ones that we embody in dynamic interplay, working together for our good and wholeness. Wholeness, then, is not about becoming perfect. It is meeting and accepting our true selves. And because we are ever-changing beings, actively working toward harmonizing these aspects of ourselves is what it means to be truly awake and alive.

While so much of what we find in our personal descents into the teeming underworld is individualized—unique experiences, histories, and struggles—as we journey through this abyss, we find the Mother leading us down deeper to the source of our shared internal pain. If we look carefully, with time we begin to see that our collective wounding begins as a point of basic confusion about our natures as divine children of heavenly parents. Generations of false traditions have spread confusion around the true nature of the divine femininity and the divine masculinity They embody.

Since the beginning, the fruit of this wound has been and continues to be unrighteous dominion, systematized in the world as patriarchy. Patriarchy—a social system and hierarchical structure in which men hold primary power and predominate in political leadership, moral authority, social privilege, and control of property—has shaped our views of women and men for millennia.[15] It is the fabric and face of every hierarchical social, political, and economic structure, and our greatest root of discord. Placing oneself above another was the first sin story.[16] In the world of government and commerce, we come up against the reality that "we wrestle not against flesh and blood, but against principalities, against powers, against the rulers of the darkness of this world, against spiritual wickedness in high places."[17] Because they rely on inequality, hierarchical structures of power cannot survive in Zion. Love cannot prevail in any instance in which an individual desires to maintain control. Where Zion is, so are the "pure in heart"—souls fully committed to egalitarianism, shared property, and care for the least of these.

Patriarchy doesn't only disenfranchise women. It subjugates anyone who does not fit the narrow definition of "worthy" by the few upholding power. Patriarchal masculinity estranges boys and men from their selfhood as much as patriarchal femininity estranges girls and women from their selfhood, just in different ways. It demands that men hold power *above* rather than *with*, keeping them from loving with all of themselves. Through the media, patriarchy tells us on a daily basis that men in power are able to do whatever they desire, and that that freedom is what makes them men. Patriarchal masculinity requires boys and men to uphold ideals of manhood that get in the way of loving justice between a woman and a man. The solution to this imbalance, as we know, is the perfectly just love of Jesus the Christ. As bell hooks, cultural critic and feminist theorist, puts it so poignantly in her book *All About Love*, "Loving justice for themselves and others enables men to break the chokehold of patriarchal masculinity."[18]

Jesus embodied attributes of divine masculinity *and* divine femininity. Among those men in Israel who wielded corrupt power, the scribes and Pharisees of His day, He compared Himself to a mother hen desiring to gather her chicks.[19] Was He rejected because of His resemblance to the Mother? His consistent appeal to the world to embrace feminine aspects of deity—compassion, nurture, unity, intuition, community—not only left him quite friendless but also made him an enemy to the institutions that harbored contempt for any teachings that would suggest the prostitute was equal to the priest. He sacrificed His life for the truth of humankind's equality before God. Giving Himself over to death, He was received into the arms of the Mother, She who discerns and nurtures in the underworld and who co-reigns over the re-creative forces of the cosmos. He offers healing and wholeness to us as a connective bridge between heaven and earth, through which our souls pass into the arms of our Mother and Father to rest eternally.

Our Origin Story

To help us examine some of the oldest beliefs we hold about our relationships to each other, we begin at the beginning. Our creation story as recorded in Genesis is mythic in its portent and power over the Judeo-Christian mind. It imbues all creation with purpose and meaning. Some of these meanings are derived from our human frailty and limitations. If we look closely, we find the story fraught with misconceptions and troubling words—*beguiled*, *rule over*, *rib*—imperfect translations with missing pieces. Shifts in perception and values, specifically about gender equality, color the lens through which we interpret and internalize Eve's discerning and her understanding of her choices. Our relationship to each other and all of creation, how we reach for the divine in the wilderness of mortality, hinges on that internalization.

To open the fabric of the narrative, I share a portion of our creation story from my vantage point as a woman. It is a glimpse into how I have come to read the story, a suggestion of what it may have been like to see as Eve—humanity's female archetype—and to see the Mother in the Garden of Eden, how She influenced the choices made there. I anchor my interpretation in various scriptural accounts, from which I call on my intuition and my spiritual guides to work as a compass inside me. Creating a retelling of the creation story is an exercise in engagement with scripture as *living* writ. These sacred tellings are resources for our interaction and growth, but we bring meaning to them; their meanings are not fixed in time.

The creation story is so familiar that sometimes we are not able to hear it. With this retelling, notice the questions that arise in you, and ponder how your faith journey meets the creation story and how we might make room together for more truth.

When the world is formed, it is empty and desolate.[20] Chaos prevails, and the Gods move over the waters, listening. Listening blooms power so that when They speak, the words in Their mouths are full of love. Purpose finds its way to Their tongues, and the words become song: "Let there be" becomes light. And because the Gods comprehend the light, They can name it and shape it. And discern it from the dark. All its properties and purposes. And this is how day becomes a companion to night and everything They speak comes into being.

They sing, and the firmament divides from the waters. And within the moving light of heaven, morning is born and the evening and the night numbered; time is born. They organize the lights in the expanse of heaven for signs. Sun, moon, and stars—maps and reminders to creation of Their love—revolving light bodies cycling seasons, days, and years. And the Gods watch as every atom to which They sing and pray awakes and yields to the great melody of joy. And because of this joy, all creation listens.[21]

The Gods sing the land dry and sing the great waters together. In the great divisions, a way is opened to abundance, to creatures in the firmament, the land, and the sea. And the Gods bless every part and portion, every whale and every blade of grass.

‘Adam—human beings—are imagined[22] by the Gods.[23] From this oneness, also, the Gods see purpose in division. Man is formed first from the red clay of Earth, and so called Adam.[24] Housed in the garden temple of Eden, he is told of the power of the tree of knowledge of good and evil before the feminine is housed in flesh. Before the feminine and the masculine divide. He is told not to partake of this power, not to eat its fruit.

A deep sleep moves through Adam. He sees in vision the foretold separation, the feminine organized, transposed into woman.[25] As They sang the land from the water, and the day from the night, the Gods sing the female and male apart and shape them.[26]

They emerge as distinct forms. Eve, one half of a whole, a fashioned, differentiated soul. Adam forgets what it was to be whole and senses a profound longing within his new body, his mind, and heart that he can't articulate but feels fulfilled in the presence of Eve. She becomes his balancing, centering life force. She becomes his axis mundi, his tree of life.

Eve, who was not instructed not to eat the fruit, is free to express her innate knowing, the newfound wisdom of her embodiment—mind, heart, flesh—incapable of denying the powers of creation inside her cells, singing for expansion. Adam, separate from the creative ordinances of Eve, waits.

Midmost in the Garden, planted above the four cardinal rivers, the tree of life[27] sings. Veiled behind the tree of knowledge, She whispers, rustles Her leaves as Eve opens her heart and listens: What is eternal life without discernment? What is knowledge without wisdom? Eve comes to the branches encircling the tree of life. There, the serpent twines on the hedge.

She sees the tree of life through the veil: Her ancient girth and canopy spread greater than any ever seen. Grooved deeply with the slow expansion of eons, She is home to colonies of lichen and carpets of moss draping Her long limbs. Owls and ravens sleep in Her most shadowed boughs. There is recognition, resonance pulsing between the spirit of the tree and the spirit of Eve. See the tree and see the Mother, sovereign and consequential, ruling and reigning in the eternities.

In that realm of awakening enters the serpent. Satan's mimetic form in the Garden intends to derail the purpose of the Gods but comes before Eve disguised as a symbol of salvation, an image of the Christ.[28] Symbol of fertility and creative life force. Of rebirth, transformation, immortality, and healing.[29] A symbol that speaks to Eve of her generative powers. Eve stares at the scene, recognizing the mirror placed, the path forward as her own body, opened, the mysteries of creation her birthright: she is looking at herself. Her eyes open before the tree and the serpent. Her vision of herself unfolds.

Eve, a veil. Eve, a tree of life. Eve, the embodied way to mortal life and death. She sees the tree and sees the Mother and Son and sees herself and sees the serpent and sees the Mother and Son and sees herself. Endless circle. She steps toward the veiling hedge, desiring to reach her Mother.

Created in the image of the Mother, Eve embodies the feminine aspects of human consciousness, a honed sensitivity to the interconnectedness of all things. She knows that seeds (of plants, of the womb) must bear fruit, that some fruits fall to the earth without flowering, that some seeds emerge as trees that hold up the world. In this green new garden, she senses the need for good and evil, interconnection and separation, for paradox, for opposition, for all things being a compound in one.[30] From this place, she chooses the path, puts together the mental and emotional puzzle, the if/then of salvation and survival. She comprehends the paradox: to become as the Gods, we must leave Them. To bind up our hearts and wills to Them, we must move out from under Their care. To be one with Them and all of creation—one with ourselves finally—we have to live for a space in a state of woundedness. She sinks her teeth into the fruit.

As we see in various scripture stories, visionary states are induced by divine figures to reveal divine purposes. I imagine the deep sleep of Adam closing his heart, mind, and body to the realm of the woman who would part from his side. I see him instructed on the necessity of being sundered in order for life to truly begin, for the work of mortality to commence. For the womb to have its reign. For the feminine creative powers to be accepted or rejected by humankind as the necessary first step toward agency. Each human soul who would follow would choose to heal or further divide this first separation of the feminine and masculine.

In Genesis, Moses, and the Book of Abraham, the man Adam, spirit and element, receives instruction from the Gods not to partake of the fruit of the tree of knowledge of good and evil *before* Eve is created and housed in flesh. I believe that this element is underemphasized and exposes a crucial theological gap, which is that Eve is an independent source of agency and discernment in the Garden. If it is true that God did not instruct Eve not to partake of the fruit, then the instruction would have come through Adam, and God would have made that choice for a reason. God knew what would unfold, and God knew that Eve was capable of using her knowledge of the plan of salvation, her bodily intuition and spiritual gifts, to determine a path forward for the children she would bring into the world. Her creative desires and wisdom have long been denigrated by Christian theologians, which has created suspicion about women's role in the Church that is completely unwarranted. With the tree of life planted in the Garden, Eve would have felt the influence of the Mother, a guide on the path to mortality and Eve's role as Mother of All Living.

While we know from Genesis 3 and Moses 4[31] that she is aware of the command and its source, the order of events from these accounts asks us to consider Adam separate from the authority of Eve and from the creative ordinances of women. The ordinances of women include ordinances of embodiment. As Valerie Hudson puts it so beautifully, "The word *ordinance* means a physical act with deep spiritual meaning. So certainly pregnancy, childbirth, [and] lactation are all ordinances of the gospel. They cannot be otherwise. They are clearly the priestesshood ordinances presided over by women."[32] Surely Eve, as Mother of All Living, presided over the ordinances of embodiment and had knowledge from the Mother to make her decision.

Was it possible, then, for the Gods to ask Eve to go against herself and the very purpose of her creation?

As many scholars have described, the structure of the ancient Israelite temples mirrors the layout of the Garden of Eden. Michael A. Fishbane, American scholar of Judaism and rabbinic literature, describes the Garden as "an axis mundi. From it radiate primal streams to the four quarters. . . . It is the navel or omphalos," and the tree of life is situated at "the center of this center."[33] Jeffrey M. Bradshaw explains how Ezekiel 28:13 locates Eden on the mountain of God.[34] As a cosmic mountain, Eden is an archetype for the earthly temple. Isaiah describes the Jerusalem temple as "the mountain of the Lord's house."[35] It is, therefore, identified, like Eden, as a symbol of the center.[36]

The Zohar, the chief text of the Jewish Kabbalah, describes the tree of life in the exact middle of the Garden. It goes on to say that the tree of knowledge of good and evil was not exactly in the middle.[37] Bradshaw explains that "an interesting Jewish tradition about the placement of the two trees is the idea that the foliage of the tree of knowledge hid the tree of life from direct view" and that "God did not specifically prohibit eating from the tree of life because the tree of knowledge formed a hedge around it; only after one had partaken of the latter and cleared a path for herself could one come close to the tree of life."[38] Bradshaw continues:

> Consistent with this Jewish tradition about the placement of the trees and the scholarship that sees the Garden of Eden as a temple prototype, Ephrem the Syrian, a fourth-century Christian, called the tree of knowledge "the veil of the sanctuary." He pictured Paradise as a great mountain, with the tree of knowledge providing a permeable boundary partway up the slopes. The tree

> of knowledge, Ephrem concluded, "acts as a sanctuary curtain [i.e., veil] hiding the Holy of Holies, which is the Tree of Life higher up." In addition to this inner boundary, Jewish, Christian, and Muslim sources sometimes speak of a "wall" surrounding the whole of the garden, separating it from the "outer court" of our mortal world.[39]

It is possible to see Eve as not fully awake to the divine. She comes to the grove of trees and then sees the tree of life, the Mother Tree through that veil. The veil implies some obscuring of vision. Perhaps she doesn't have a perfect understanding, but she does know the way forward. She trusts herself. She understands the power of her agency in the tapestry of her own transformation. As Jewish teacher and spiritual leader Yiskah Rosenfeld notes, Eve "undertakes the most radical and subversive act of all: changing herself."[40]

The serpent is rich in complicated polarities. Scholars show that "the image of the snake or serpent in the ancient world was a dual symbol representing deity, creativity, and healing on the one hand, but evil, harm, and destruction on the other."[41] Through the scriptures, we also find the serpent symbolizing both harm and healing, as demonstrated in the story of Moses and the children of Israel.[42] When they sin in the wilderness, and are bitten by fiery serpents, Moses makes a brass image of a serpent for the people to look at. Those who look are healed. This healing image points us to Jehovah, the Savior, who is the salvation from death. John 3:14–15 gives us the interpretation: "And as Moses lifted up the serpent in the wilderness, even so must the Son of man be lifted up: That whosoever believeth in him should not perish, but have eternal life." We see that "according to Jesus, the serpent was intended to be the supernal symbol of Himself and His atonement."[43]

Eve recognizes both salvation and danger in the serpent's presence. While Satan came with ulterior motives, the message he communicated to Eve rang true: that the path to godhood was a path of reconciliation. That Eve, Mother of All Living, would act as a savior to all the souls of humanity by becoming the vessel through which life began (and thus also death), birthing us into the mortal world, which would allow us to enter into the way of transformation. While Satan has no power to offer what he did—"Ye shall not surely die; . . . ye shall be as gods"[44]—Eve recognizes not only the Savior and His role in salvation in the duality of the serpent symbol, but she also sees herself, her fertility, her creative powers in commencing the workings of life and death intrinsic to salvation. She offers embodied life that would lead to death but that would then lead to life everlasting in Christ. Life-death-life. Eternal, like Ouroboros.[45] I believe Eve recognized partnership with Adam in bringing souls to Earth and partnership with Christ in saving them.

How does it change our feelings and perspective of women to consider them as saviors in the world, touching heaven as they touch Earth, sacred veils bringing souls into mortality who otherwise could not progress?

I offer this reading in the hope that it may contrast with some of the more prevalent interpretations and narratives that weave through our inherited roots, ones that biblical language allows, such as the following: because of Eve, we are sinful and fallen. Foolishly, she listened to the serpent, and because of that wrong choice, the world suffers. Many members of the

Church believe that Eve's choice in Eden to partake of the fruit was a good choice. Yet, the narrative that she wrongfully instigated humanity's fall through disobedience (whether as a mythical character or literal woman) lies at the heart of the larger Judeo-Christian interpretation and is used to excuse the subjugation of women: to justify the belief that women are fundamentally inadequate in their decision-making powers, dependent on men to guide and teach them, and quite literally not made to be sovereign agents. Of the forty times *tsela* is used in the Bible, it is only translated as "rib" in the story of Eve's creation.[46] How quickly this image of woman as rib is misconstrued to mean women are appendages of men—a part, a portion, made solely for the purpose of supporting a man in his journey—rather than fully formed, independent, autonomous beings.

Addressing the confusion and collective root rot regarding the feminine and the masculine begins with an examination of the ways in which Eve and Adam are depicted. For me, questioning why and how certain attributes have been assigned to Eve has been a good starting point. This requires going back to the origins of how this story was recorded and disseminated and acknowledging the layers of interpretation through which this story in particular has passed, as well-intentioned as translators could have been.[47] Those who wrote down the earliest renditions of the creation story and translated them were men.[48] Those who decided which stories should constitute the Bible were men. Those who codified and largely interpreted the creation story for our Latter-day Saint doctrine and theology were men. Our views are limited to the masculine lens because of this disproportionate influence. The absence of women's voices and experiences in our canon reflects the limitations we have placed on the voice and presence of women in our language and in our religious framing of what is sacred and real.

Original Wound

A vision of healthy femininity and healthy masculinity is fundamental to our journeys back home. Satan, the Destroyer, dominates in the world by corrupting humanity's relationship to feminine and masculine principles. He has led the charge to distort what those authentic ways truly are. His counternarrative, one based on discord, is woven throughout the fabric of human society and the hierarchical structures of institutions that place select men in power above all others.

Historically, the urge to dominate, control, and own has been systematized by men. Our own scriptures teach us that "it is the nature and disposition of *almost all men*, as soon as they get a little authority, as they suppose, they will immediately begin to exercise unrighteous dominion."[49] Observing this assumption of power over another and noting how it became established as a historical process, scholars believe that patriarchy developed from 3100 BCE to 600 BCE in the Near East and has thrived ever since. It is believed that patriarchy arose partly from the practice of intertribal exchanges of women for marriage "in which women acquiesced because it was functional for the tribe."[50] As the basic system of society or government in which men hold power and women are excluded from that power, patriarchy is the model of organization wherein males and all things associated with masculinity are valued over things associated with women and femininity. Patriarchy teaches that men are more valuable than women, "that productive work is more important than reproductive work, and that caregiving and nurturing are women's work (and therefore, less valuable)."[51]

The toxic power structure of a culture that sees primarily through a masculine lens creates suspicions and fear of what would challenge it, namely what the rational mind cannot perceive, touch, or analyze. Hyperrationality minimizes the importance of other ways of knowing and creating meaning. It often discounts the necessary place of the ineffable in knowledge creation, the power of the unknown and unknowable. The spaces in between. The masculine striving toward achievement, production, and control becomes valued above the feminine qualities of relatedness—"relatedness to other humans, to the non-humans who share the planet with us, to nature and the rhythms of nature, as well as to the rhythms of the physical body and the stages and passages of our lives."[52] The complete failure of this artificial division in ways of knowing is made even more apparent by empirical research findings revealing that humans are emotional actors who respond first from intuition, and only after our response do we work overtime to find rational justification.[53] Men often diminish women for using emotion and intuition to inform their decisions while at the same time asserting that men do not use emotions to inform theirs. Both women and men have been separated from important ways of relating to themselves and each other. The tendency to consciously and unconsciously disassociate from the more intuitive aspects of ourselves can cause real harm to our sense of reality, a harm that ripples from individuals into institutions, policies, and practices.

In the Church, we have unwittingly inherited a reading of patriarchy onto Eve and Adam's story, beginning with the idea that Eve's feminine way of knowing was inherently flawed. For generations, the explicit cause and effect of Eve's choice was in our own temple language: Eve transgressed, so Adam had to reconcile Eve's disobedience with God; therefore, God gave Adam direction to lead Eve. It took until the year 2019 for this ingrained notion and false tradition to be rescinded and dismantled, righting our theology. This allowed the truth to be known that men never were and never could be intermediaries between women and God in the temple or anywhere, ever.[54]

We are all at different places in our understanding of the painful realities of patriarchy. Patriarchal ideology is so pervasive that many believe that following its ideals is the only way to manage societies and organizations. It is called "benevolent patriarchy" because at first glance it appears to be a natural fact of life, one that is for everyone's good. For women who have come to grasp the effects of patriarchy in our lives, though, our experience looks something like this: We realize we've spent years masking the powerful parts of ourselves that challenge the stability of patriarchy. We learned how to navigate, how to speak the language of fawning and submission, how to adapt. Through stings and snubs, jokes and barbs, we learned that what we have to say is considered less valuable than what men say, and we ended up believing it is true. We discover that in patriarchy many women have not only lost their voice but also that many remain asleep to what sovereignty they have lost, having never experienced full self-determination, and thus not knowing what could be. When we begin to express ourselves by calling for moral or ethical correction in an individual, an institution, or a community, these calls are often silenced, ignored, or met with threats. We learn that the roles of women are largely crafted by men and that these roles are reductive, since it is impossible for men to accurately understand the lives of women. We are told, in direct and indirect ways, that we shouldn't follow our dreams because we are women. We learn that our joyful bodies are a target. When we radiate our God-given sensuality, we are a target. We find visceral reminders in the news of how women's daily existence, necessary self-protection, and resistance to control is often met with violence, overwhelmingly from their male partners.[55] We know that the loss of women's sovereignty is linked to the loss of Mother Earth's sovereignty.[56]

Part of the delusion of the patriarchal world is the belief that the masculine encompasses all of the feminine, that what it defines as feminine is merely an extension of the male world.[57] In extreme cases of patriarchy's influence, men have largely forgotten the feminine energy inside them and that a separate female realm exists. That even momentarily in childhood, they were a part of that realm with their mothers. Their privileged position keeps them from understanding the world of subjugated women. Under the assumptions of patriarchy—that women have no equal and independent purpose or realm—men in these systems have made women, like land, literal property under the law. Women in half of the world are still denied land

and property rights despite current laws.[58] The ways in which women continue to be seen as possessions range from the obvious trophy wife trope to more subtle and nuanced ways in which women are expected to service the needs of male-dominated institutions and cater to established social norms.

Patriarchy commodifies women and does so by removing them from any profitable realm of influence and using them to prop up its values in the one sphere in which they are somewhat allowed: the home. Because patriarchy poisons this one realm of influence with the notion that women are created to remain inside its walls, the true influence women could have in society is limited by the simple, pernicious notion that what women have to say does not apply outside the walls of the home. Nor do men see the need to create policies within society that support the life-giving work of the home. In the United States, policies that support childbirth and childrearing, contraception, and adequate maternal and paternal leave are gravely inadequate if not absent. Women's real needs are silenced and relegated to insignificance instead of being prioritized as a matter of life and death.

It is difficult to look at the ways in which the patriarchal structure of our Church also limits women's involvement, but we must enter into that pain as well. Women are largely without decision-making power and leadership positions within the Church. Even a Relief Society president cannot receive revelation about who to call within her own presidency without her choice potentially being overruled by a man. Women are given many responsibilities in the Church but no authority. And we shouldn't conflate the two. A woman does not have final say on any decision in the Church. There is little room in the system of patriarchy, inside and outside the Church, for women as whole beings, full participants, as they try to bring seats to the table.

We, Latter-day Saints, have countless opportunities to change the way we see each other as we continue to reevaluate our hearts; we are confronted with those opportunities because we are woven into the same social fabric. The integration of the realm of the feminine is vital at all levels of community and society in order to rebalance the world. This rebalancing involves respect for women, their voices, their healing powers, and their work. It also involves opening a real space for the feminine to arise in us individually. Our wrestling with the current reality of male primacy and the consequential disenfranchisement of all others will lead to massive changes in how we organize family, community, and institutions, including religious ones.

Healing Together

> *When angels speak of love they tell us it is only by loving that we enter an earthly paradise. They tell us paradise is our home and love our true destiny.*[59]
>
> —bell hooks

As with the root systems of trees, our identity is largely formed in the connections we make in community. We begin our lives nurtured in the soil surrounding us. It is here in this kind of tomb and womb space where we call on the collective wisdom of our ancestors and the communities who nourished them. While the traditions we inherit can be poisonous and destructive, we also have good ancestral traditions and blessings that come to us. We have spiritual ancestors who we seek to emulate—people who, like King Lamoni's wife, climbed out of hell and touched heaven. We have to look downward and backward into that underworld to contact their stories as well.

In our need for a sense of continuity, the Divine Feminine shows us that the wisdom of our ancestors is still available, still a part of our cells. Their understanding of the complexities of mortal life—tending the land, finding patience in grief and frailty, recognizing how deeply connected we all are—is available to us through the channels of familial bonds. They call out for us to continue on the journey toward wholeness. Their offering of collective wisdom feeds our growth and ascent.

I felt this living connection to my Knight ancestors while serving as a missionary in Italy. During my first few months, I experienced something I never thought I could: a prolonged distancing from God. It was excruciating. While my testimony deepened and I progressed with Italian, I struggled every day with feeling spiritually abandoned. I had no reason to feel so tormented because of anything I had done relating to the worthiness standards of the Church. At the time I didn't realize what was happening: that my feelings of despair were not rooted in sin but necessary for the next stage of my spiritual transformation. I kept going. I had to; there was no other way.

I shared the first lesson about the Restoration to many at that time. But in Livorno, while teaching a young Italian man whose sister was recently baptized, I suddenly, like the unexpected presence of the Spirit, felt the presence of my Knight ancestors. As I spoke of them, the distance in time and space between us collapsed. I felt them in my cells, in my heart, and in my mind. With their love of the gospel filling my whole being, the work of restoration was alive in me as their progeny and as a missionary continuing what they had begun. They were among the first converts in New York and supported the work of the early Restoration at great personal sacrifice. Their devotion to the gospel of Christ had planted in me as a child an abiding connection to the power and reality of the prophetic mantle of Joseph Smith and the vision of Zion they loved. When I remembered them in that moment, they answered the deepest longings and love in my heart for the work of my Savior. Even more tenderly for me, they answered my need to feel loved and seen in that almost impossible time.

We can call on our ancestors, our female ancestors, especially when we need help healing the wounded feminine inside us. As we heal, they heal in turn. This can look like simply accepting and setting the intention in prayer to receive what they have to communicate.

Descending into the darkness is entering into feminine territory. Perhaps only Jesus completes this descent because of the way He harmonizes the feminine and masculine powers of deity inside Him. In His atonement and death He completely surrendered in vulnerability to the unknown. Jesus comprehends all things, and I believe He learned from His Mother how to go down into the depths and be refined by them. Adding our Mother to the equation of salvation means we choose to surrender to the mystery of becoming in its multitude of manifestations. Our path is not just one of religious demarcation, of checking off performative markers of progression, but, as Jesus taught—and as I believe He learned in unique ways from His Mother—of soul-making, of soul-expansion.

We don't enter the underworld just once; if we remain open to our Mother's call, we will cycle down as many times as we are asked, to generate deeper wisdom and deeper levels of trust in the divine and deeper degrees of healing the wounded feminine. The heart must break open again and again to incorporate and integrate bodily, earth-bound wisdom gathered in the cells and strata of our beings. In a world where we are consistently wounded by distortions of worthiness, this radical commitment to transformation is the way we live the profound intuition of the body and spirit to discern our reality and move in the power of divine love.

NOTES

1 Peter Wohlleben, *The Hidden Life of Trees* (London: Williams Collins, 2017), 82.

2 Wohlleben, *Hidden Life of Trees*, 81.

3 Wohlleben, *Hidden Life of Trees*, 83.

4 Wohlleben, *Hidden Life of Trees*, 171.

5 Wohlleben, *Hidden Life of Trees*, 171.

6 Suzanne Simard, *Finding the Mother Tree: Discovering the Wisdom of the Forest* (New York: Alfred A. Knopf, 2021), 5.

7 Wohlleben, *Hidden Life of Trees*, 34.

8 Christine Caine, *Unashamed: Drop the Baggage, Pick up Your Freedom, Fulfill Your Destiny* (Grand Rapids, MI: Zondervan, 2016), 160.

9 From a letter to the Church signed by Joseph Smith Jr. and four others on March 20, 1839, from Liberty Jail, Clay County, Missouri.

10 Clarissa Pinkola Estés, *Women Who Run with the Wolves: Myths and Stories of the Wild Woman Archetype* (New York: Ballantine Books, 1992), 33.

11 "Each of us must turn inward and destroy in himself all that he thinks he ought to destroy in others. And remember that every atom of hate we add to this world makes it still more inhospitable." Etty Hillesum, *Etty: The Letters and Diaries of Etty Hillesum* 1941–1943 (Grand Rapids, MI: B. Eerdmans, 2002), 529.

12 Rainer Maria Rilke, "Pushing Through," in *Selected Poems of Rainer Maria Rilke*, trans. and ed. Robert Bly (New York: Harper and Row, 1981), 55.

13 Proverbs 26:11.

14 "If men do not comprehend the character of God, they do not comprehend themselves." Joseph Smith Jr., "The King Follett Sermon."

15 Robert Bahlieda, "Chapter 1: The Legacy of Patriarchy," *Counterpoints* 488 (2015): 15–67, http://www.jstor.org/stable/45136330.

16 The murder of Abel by Cain. See Genesis 4:1–16.

17 Ephesians 6:12.

18 bell hooks, *All About Love* (New York: HarperCollins, 2001), 42.

19 See Matthew 23:37.

20 Abraham 4:2.

21 "Since both plant and animal life are living souls, they are capable of experiencing happiness as they fulfill the measure of their creation." Marcus B. Nash, "Righteous Dominion and Compassion for the Earth" (speech, 18th Annual Stegner Center Symposium, Salt Lake City, UT, April 12, 2013).

22 Book of Abraham 3.

23 "The term 'adam . . . is a generic term for human beings, not a proper noun. It also does not automatically suggest maleness, especially not without the prefix ben, 'son of,' and so the traditional rendering 'man' is misleading, and an exclusively male 'adam would make nonsense of the last clause of verse 27." Robert Alter, *The Five Books of Moses: A Translation with Commentary* (New York: W. W. Norton 2004), 19.

24 The personal name Adam derives from the Hebrew noun adamah, meaning "the ground" or "earth." Adam (אדם) literally means "red," and there is an etymological connection between *adam* and *adamah, adamah* designating "red clay" or "red ground" in a nontheological context. In traditional Jewish theology, a strong etymological connection between the two words is often assumed.

25 My personal feeling is that Eve and Adam represent ends of a continuum between what we term feminine and masculine. In addition to being real people, they are representatives of the feminine and masculine components of the personal psyche of each reader.

26 *Tsela*: Hebrew for "side" as well as "rib," as in one of two sides or one of two halves. "And the Lord God . . . took one of his ribs, and closed up the flesh instead thereof; and the rib, which the Lord God had taken from man, made he a woman, and brought her unto the man" (Genesis 2:21–22).

27 The tree of life is synonymous with the Mother Tree here. The tree of life in the Garden of Eden is the same tree that Lehi and Nephi saw, known as the love of God. See 1 Nephi 11:22.

28 "And as Moses lifted up the serpent in the wilderness, even so must the Son of man be lifted up: That whosoever believeth in him should not perish, but have eternal life" (John 3:14–15).

29 Andrew C. Skinner, "Serpent Symbols and Salvation in the Ancient Near East and the Book of Mormon," *Journal of Book of Mormon Studies* 10, no. 2 (2001): 44, https://scholarsarchive.byu.edu/jbms/vol10/iss2/8.

30 2 Nephi 2:11.

31 Genesis 3:2; Moses 4:9.

32 Valerie Hudson, "Women in the Church—A Conversation with Valerie Hudson," *Faith Matters*, December 29, 2019, https://faithmatters.org/women-in-the-church-a-conversation-with-valerie-hudson/.

33 Michael A. Fishbane, "The Sacred Center," in *Texts and Responses: Studies Presented to Nahum H. Glatzer on the Occasion of His Seventieth Birthday by His Students*, ed. Michael A. Fishbane and P. R. Flohr (Leiden, Netherlands: Brill, 1975), 9.

34 Jeffrey M. Bradshaw, "The Tree of Knowledge as the Veil of the Sanctuary," in *Ascending the Mountain of the Lord: Temple, Praise, and Worship in the Old Testament* (2013 Sperry Symposium), ed. Jeffrey R. Chadwick, Matthew J. Grey, and David Rolph Seely (Provo, UT: Religious Studies Center, Brigham Young University; Salt Lake City: Deseret Book, 2013), 49–65.

35 Isaiah 2:2.

36 Bradshaw, "Tree of Knowledge," 49–65.

37 Bradshaw, "Tree of Knowledge," 49–65.

38 Bradshaw, "Tree of Knowledge," 49–65.

39 Bradshaw, "Tree of Knowledge," 49–65.

40 Yiskah Rosenfeld, "You Take Lilith, I'll Take Eve: A Closer Look at the World's Second Feminist," in *Yentl's Revenge: The Next Wave of Jewish Feminism*, ed. Danya Ruttenberg (Seattle: Seal Press, 2001).

41 W. S. McCullough, "Serpent," in *The Interpreter's Dictionary of the Bible* (New York: Abingdon, 1962), 4:290. See also the succeeding article in the same volume: L. Hicks, "Serpent, Bronze," 291.

42 See Numbers 21:4–9.

43 Skinner, "Serpent Symbols and Salvation," 50.

44 Moses 4:7, 10–11.

45 Ouroboros is an ancient symbol of a snake or a dragon consuming its own tail. It represents eternal, cyclical renewal to some and a cycle of life, death, and rebirth to others.

46 The English translation of tsela as "rib" instead of one of Adam's two "sides," or one of the two "halves" of the bilateral first human, was standardized by Wycliffe in the King James Version of the Bible and has become entrenched in most English Bibles (Genesis 2:21–22). See John H. Walton, *The Lost World of Adam and Eve* (London: InterVarsity Press, 2015), 78.

47 There are multiple layers of interpretation through which biblical texts, and specifically the creation story from Genesis, pass before they reach our ears. Our job is to feel out—with the help of the Spirit, our intuition, and hearts—what settles with our understanding of the nature of our divine parents and what does not. This is a journey of a lifetime; our views will continue to shift, our powers of discernment will become refined, and our wisdom will increase. A fluidity toward how we read the text, then, would best serve us.

48 There is significant evidence that the creation story in Genesis comes from three different texts, referred to as the "J," "E," and "P" texts by scholars.

49 Doctrine and Covenants 121:39; emphasis added.

50 Glenn Collins, "Patriarchy: Is It Invention or Inevitable?" *New York Times*, April 28, 1986, https://www.nytimes.com/1986/04/28/style/patriarchy-is-it-invention-or-inevitable.html#:~:text=Lerner%20views%20the%20establishment%20of,was%20functional%20for%20the%20tribe.

51 Dr. Julie Hanks, Instagram, https://www.instagram.com/p/CMXfm SSHYU-/.

52 Sharon Blackie, *If Women Rose Rooted: A Life-Changing Journey to Authenticity and Belonging* (Tewkesbury, UK: September, 2019), 245.

53 See Jonathan Haidt, *The Righteous Mind: Why Good People Are Divided by Politics and Religion* (New York: Vintage, 2013).

54 Jana Riess, "Major Changes to Mormon Temple Ceremony, Especially for Women," *Religion News Service*, January 3, 2019, https://religionnews.com/2019/01/03/major-changes-to-mormon-temple-ceremony-especially-for-women/.

55 United Nations Office on Drugs and Crime, *Global Study on Homicide: Gender-Related Killing of Women and Girls*, 2018, https://www.unodc.org/documents/data-and-analysis/GSH2018/GSH18_Gender-related_killing_of_women_and_girls.pdf.

56 For a more in-depth look at the connection between the treatment of the earth and the treatment of women, see Kathryn Knight Sonntag, "The Mother Tree: Understanding the Spiritual Root of Our Ecological Crisis," in *Dialogue: A Journal of Mormon Thought* 52, no. 1 (Spring 2019), 17.

57 "Women suffer from greater rates of anxiety and depression, [and poor] self-worth compared to men starting at puberty. This is directly related to the objectification of women's bodies and patriarchy's notion that women (and their bodies) belong to men." Dr. Julie Hanks, Instagram, https://www.instagram.com/p/CMXfmSSHYU-/.

58 "Women in Half the World Still Denied Land, Property Rights Despite Laws," press release, The World Bank, March 25, 2019, https://www.worldbank.org/en/news/press-release/2019/03/25/women-in-half-the-world-still-denied-land-property-rights-despite-laws.

59 hooks, *All About Love*, 237.

CHAPTER TWO

Trunk

Earth: Through All Things

If we focus on the tree in our mind's eye, the upright and striking form of its physical presence comes forth. Its vertical line moves our eyes upward to the fruit and leaves of its branches, to the skies above. The trunk is the main organ of the tree. Its rigid woody structure provides the central support for all that happens to the tree. It supports the crown and functions as a conduit, carrying water and minerals up from the ground and transporting sugars from the leaves to feed the root system.

The bark of the trunk protects the living tissue from damage by the elements, animals, bacteria, and fungi, but this armor isn't without feeling or sensitivity. Tree trunks can register light. "Most tree species have tiny dormant buds nestled in their bark"[1] that receive light waves and can sense the amount of daylight available to the tree, thereby orienting it in time by length of days even when its branches are bare.

The trunk comprises four layers: heartwood, xylem, cambium, and phloem. Heartwood is the hard core, made up of old xylem layers that have died and become compressed by the newer outer layers. The xylem is also called sapwood and carries water and minerals up the trunk. The cambium is a thin layer where new cells develop to either become xylem, phloem, or more cambium. A cambium layer is turned into xylem once each year, creating an annual ring around the trunk. Just outside the cambium, the phloem moves sugars from the leaves down to the roots. As it dies, the phloem forms the bark.

Looking back at our diagram, we see that the trunk of the archetypal tree represents the mortal sphere. Here, we rise up and manifest new ways of being from the feelings and beliefs we cultivate in our cycles of descent. The intuition, impressions, and visions nurtured in the chambers of the soul come to be birthed—to gain physicality and form in the visible world. In community and communion, new patterns of interaction emerge. We learn how to love more fully from a heart nurtured and, thus, open, in healthy vulnerability.

The vertical axis of the trunk symbolizes a bridge between our fledgling knowledge and the divine wisdom in the heavens above. Our earth-bound wisdom is gathered in the realm of the trunk, which leads us to celestial understandings. So while, in our root work, we strive to relieve our souls of things that may cause harm, we are always in the process of uncovering our true selves, of moving toward wholeness and greater understanding—reckoning at the roots that affects the health of our trunk and branches. As we continue to access the healing powers of the divine, we see more and more clearly the reality of our lives.

In this way, Mother God teaches that "wisdom is not knowing more, but knowing with more of you, knowing deeper."[2] Tapping into divinely feminine traits with the guidance of our

Mother creates a grounding and depth to our experience of the world and of ourselves. She calls us to a deeper state of awareness. Our senses become heightened. We hear more acutely and see more sincerely into the truth of all things. Importantly, we learn to trust our bodily, experiential wisdom. We begin to understand the balance of the divinely feminine and divinely masculine aspects of ourselves as we learn how the mind, spirit, and body intersect. The Mother encourages this multidimensional integration of all facets of the self, just as the tree has many interactive layers. These are complex energies that emanate from one living being to another, and they bind us together in ways that are both eternally consequential and somewhat elusive to our full understanding in mortality. As we learn to weave these different intelligences together, we come to see that we are here on Earth to deepen our souls in an act of co-creation with divinity.

Our Mother is able to help us integrate different intelligences because She is not limited to the symbolic. If we expand our view from seeing Heavenly Mother as secondary to the Father or as hidden from our view, we can see Her as Creatress. Her spirit is infused in the very fabric of creation, forever present in the living, breathing arc of life that surrounds us every moment. I have felt this holy feminine energy and presence in the natural world speaking to my soul, soothing some of my most anguished seeking. As Christ is in and through all things, the light of truth, consider how He rose to this astonishing potential. Consider His Mother's contribution to His formation and ascent. Through all things, the Mother of creation, our Mother, with our Father and Jesus, emanates from the creation of Her own hands.[3] She is present in the very dirt under our feet. From the first parting of the firmament over the land, and like the parables woven from Jesus's lips, She thrives. In the wisdom of the land She speaks. In the howl of the wolf, the quaking of tectonic plates, in the breaking down of chlorophyll, the revelation of colors long buried now vibrant, the voice of the Mother is in the wild all around us and the wild within us. We are wild, not in the word's pejorative sense meaning out of control but in its original sense: striving to live a natural life, one full of innate integrity and healthy boundaries. Living a natural life is how we could describe our acceptance of self. It means cultivating a practice of surrender to our inner knowing in order to stay grounded in what is real.

Every body is unique and will access its innate knowing differently. There are many tools to use, both physical and spiritual, to help you tap into what your body is telling you. We are taught to listen to the Spirit, but the Spirit operates through the body, and there are many signals that we may receive, telling us we are on track or that we need to fine-tune the ways we are engaging with the world. For example, it is possible to speak with our heart. Many ancient cultures know this. We can speak with our heart as if it were an intimate friend. In modern life we have become so busy with our daily activities that we have lost this essential art of taking time to converse with the heart.[4] What does your heart want you to remember? What does it need you to feel? Don't evaluate what comes up. Sit in stillness and allow the heart's wisdom to rise up above the noise of passing thoughts, above the clamor of outside stimuli. Holding yourself in kindness, not judgment, will allow your heart to reveal itself to you, whether for the first time or after a long separation. With time, you will learn how to trust it, and it will learn to trust you.

I didn't know until I was twenty-nine that my heart has its own voice. I always thought the idea of listening to one's heart was a powerful metaphor for honoring our uniquely divine essences, but I had no idea of the heart as a sort of sovereign, independent voice with its own desires of which I could be unaware. At the end of my graduate studies, a series of incredibly poignant answers to prayers and unmistakable divine direction led me back to a man I had dated two years before. The situation was more difficult this time, and part of me resisted the potential fallout if the relationship didn't ultimately work. I remember sitting next to my now husband on our second first date, watching a movie and feeling my heart speak. Over the course of a few months, it had slowly been stirring and telling me to pay attention. I've often felt the Spirit begin in this heart space, prompting words and actions, but I had never experienced my heart interjecting its own volition. This time it did. It said, *This is what we have been waiting for.*

Trunk as Axis Mundi

The trunk of the cosmic tree is the axis mundi (world axis). A vertical marker, it is the point around which the visible world revolves. It is the changeless, cosmic center. The center's inherent stillness represents entrance into divine rest in this life. In the constancy of the sacred center, we feel the presence of the sacred within the daily mundane, carrying us through strains and sorrows. Being able to feel this strength beneath the worry and desires of the moment, their projection into the past and onto the future, provides spiritual and physical orientation in the world.

Because the world axis is "the point at which all things come together," it is expressed as sacred objects and structures across the world: poles, totems, pyramids, ziggurats, and temples, to name a few.[5] These spaces are paired with sacred rituals and ceremonies that open the profane reckoning of time to a cosmic, or eternal, framing. A beautiful example of this pairing is found in the festivals that occur on May Day or Pentecost, focused around the maypole. These festivals hark back to the re-creation of the cosmos and the celebration of the changing of the seasons. The simultaneous dancing around the maypole and interweaving of colorful bands allows dancers to participate in creation—the weaving together of the world—as they symbolically reinitiate the annual experience of spring and act out a ritualized dramatization of creation. Life springs from death again and again, eternally, infinitely; the finite is made eternal.

Mother as Axis Mundi

Our own Latter-day Saint temples serve as sacred centers, world axes; they add a cosmic dimension to time ritualized, fulfilling their essential role as the conduit between heaven and earth, God and humanity. Participating in our sacred ceremonies can feel like entering the timelessness of eternity because they are designed to invoke that feeling. Our ritual partaking opens up realms of sacred time through which we are actors in the creation of the world, over and over. Through language and gestures, an effervescent union of profane and sacred realms emerges. As the Gods ordered the world of the Garden around trees that pointed to spiritual tasks that help us grow, we participate in the world of the Garden through these rituals that orient and reorient us to what matters most. While we feel a gap in our temple worship as it relates to the Mother, She was not always absent from sacred spaces. Her influence can be traced to the Garden of Eden, which was the center of the world in the beginning and the center of the Father and Mother's care for humanity.

As the Mother's body is the trunk of the tree in our chosen metaphor, we see Her image imprinted on the image of the cosmos reflected in/by many sacred spaces. Looking at the origins of our own temple worship, we find that the feminine face of the divine is rooted deeply there. In the first Jerusalem temple, "the earliest Israelites worshipped the divine mother Asherah along with the God of Israel," says Rabbi Jill Hammer.[6] As "the site of origin of divine wisdom, the means of ascent into the heavens,"[7] the world tree or world axis was recognized as Mother God. Known by many names to the Israelites, including Lady Wisdom, Shaddai, and Asherah, She spoke with the Father and the Son from the cosmological center of the Israelites: the Holy of Holies. The Holy of Holies was constructed as a perfect cube and lined with gold to represent the light and fire of the divine presence.[8] It was the heart of the temple and represented the highest order of divine power: an understanding of the mysteries of becoming.[9] It was home to the divine.

Abraham's form of temple worship was altered by King Josiah in the seventh century BCE to comply with the Book of the Law.[10] This book was discovered during the temple's renovation and is either a version of Deuteronomy or an extracanonical law code.[11] The supporters of this law code are referred to as the Deuteronomists, and their temple and worship reforms "caused the loss of what were likely many plain and precious things. Among these were the older ideas, symbols, possibly entire rituals, and forms of words from the temple as its adherents had known it, including the Lady Wisdom."[12] During the purges, every sign of the Mother in the temple, including the original menorah, was removed, burned, or destroyed.[13] In an attempt to prize written law over Wisdom and heart, the Deuteronomists did their best to erase Her from scripture, sacred spaces, and a people's shared memory.[14]

Our eminent Mother remains scant in Latter-day Saint doctrine, absent in ceremony, and hasn't been fully included in theological discourse. Yet, She is not entirely erased from scripture. "The mysterious female figure of Proverbs, Lady Wisdom, may be a version of Asherah, since she is called 'happy' (asher) and described as a tree, as Asherah was depicted as a tree."[15] Proverbs 8 reveals Her as assisting the Creator in forming the world: "When he established the heaven I was there, when he drew a circle on the face of the deep, when he made firm the skies above . . . I was beside him, like an architect [Hb., 'amon]."[16] The Greek translated *'amon as harmozousa,* meaning "the woman who holds things together" or "the woman who keeps things in tune,"[17] which implies that She was remembered as the bond of the everlasting covenant.[18]

As much as the Mother was known as the Creatress, she was also known as the retribution for covenants broken, the curse inherent in the severing of relational bonds—in harming each other—the refusal of honoring the powers of creation born from Her womb into the world. At the time of the purges, biblical scholar Margaret Barker notes, groups of believers of the older faith (such as Lehi and his family) left or were driven from Jerusalem and, in their exile, continued the older forms of Abrahamic worship.[19] These older beliefs are found in texts such as the Book of Weeks and the Apocalypse of Enoch, as well as in the Book of Mormon. Close readings of the Bible reveal evidence for the older traditions in Ezekiel, Psalms, Micah, Amos, Hosea, Jeremiah, and parts of Isaiah. Many of these prophets condemn "not only foreigners, enemies, or invaders from outside the kingdom but also the changes they saw from the religion of Abraham to that of Moses, and his Law."[20] According to Barker, "The sins of Jerusalem that Isaiah condemned were not those of the ten commandments, but those of the Enoch tradition: pride (e.g., Isa. 2:11, 17), rebellion (e.g., Isa. 1:23, 1:28, 5:24) and loss of Wisdom (e.g., Isa. 2:6, 3:12, 5:12)."[21] Chapter one of the book of Proverbs gives voice to rejected Wisdom and could well have been set in the period between the rejection of Wisdom by Josiah and the destruction of the city by the Babylonians:[22]

> How long will scoffers delight in their scoffing, and fools hate knowledge? Give heed to my reproof and I will pour out my spirit on you . . . because I called and you refused to listen . . . and you have ignored all my counsel. . . . I will laugh at your calamity, I will mock when panic strikes you

> . . . when distress and anguish come upon you. Then they will call upon me but I will not answer, they will seek me diligently but they will not find me.[23]

We see the evidence of wisdom's rejection in the Book of Mormon as well. Before we get there, let's look at some of the signs pointing us to Asherah, Lady Wisdom, in the Book of Mormon. Daniel C. Peterson, among other scholars, makes the connection between the tree of life in Lehi's vision and Asherah. Lehi and his family were contemporaries of the prophet Jeremiah who lived during the purges of the Jerusalem temple. Peterson argues that Lehi and Nephi would have known of Asherah and Her symbol as the tree of life and that this association would make sense of the instant recognition by Nephi of the tree as "the love of God." In Peterson's words, "Nephi's vision reflects a meaning of the 'sacred tree' that is unique to the ancient Near East. Asherah is . . . associated with biblical wisdom literature. Wisdom, a female, appears as the wife of God and represents life."[24]

Some of the Israelite descendants turned away from the Mother into wickedness, while others learned from Her wisdom. In Mosiah 8, King Limhi has just learned about seership and connected its absence to the children of men hardening their hearts against wisdom. Perhaps wisdom and seership were still connected in his mind. Perhaps he inherited some knowledge of Her: "O how marvelous are the works of the Lord, and how long doth he suffer with his people; yea, and how blind and impenetrable are the understandings of the children of men for they will not seek wisdom, neither do they desire that she rule over them."[25]

Our Mother is still severed from the temple, our world tree taken from our most sacred spaces—the words, gestures, and signs of the Mother in our temple missing. If She, the embodied ordinances of creation, Lady Wisdom Herself, is not at the center of our creation narrative, I wonder how we can possibly speak words with the power to bind. Although we have lost the ability to translate it, Her symbolism is still encoded in the temple narrative of the Garden. Its decoding is essential to the gathering of Israel and of truth, wherever it can be found. To prepare for the return of the Mother to the Garden, to the temple, to the center of our spiritual framing of the cosmos—to the center of our hearts—we begin by seeing Her sign separated from the signification: in the temple video and the painted walls. With a new reading of the Garden narrative, can you begin to see Her there? Even if we aren't being taught or aren't enacting the rituals about Her?[26]

It's no wonder when we don't see creation as mothered and upheld by a mother that we could make shortsighted decisions; we lack a vision of what a tree could be. And so we have made decisions systemically that have cascading unforeseen effects on our spiritual and thus physical health. It becomes evident in how our severed ideas of femininity affect our ability to properly see and understand the bodies of women.

Female Embodiment

Learning to see the Mother in the world begins with learning to love our physical bodies—their transient materiality, limitations, and pains, as well as their capacity for awe, joy, and transcendence. By listening to what they communicate, we cultivate their unique wisdom, increasing our capacity to connect with ourselves and each other in loving ways.

Reapproaching our relationship to the female body opens us to wisdom unique to the female experience and rooted in the cycles of the female body. The overly masculinized world doesn't adequately value the balancing of these cycles, which are intrinsic to our Mother and mirrored in the earth. Reverencing Her has everything to do with trusting in the mysteriousness and sacredness of these cycles. How menstruation, for example, is seen as something dirty, secret, and outside of the world demonstrates this disconnect. Disdain for and ignorance of the reproductive cycle of a woman's body, and the embarrassment women are taught to feel about their sexuality, negate the sacredness of their place as the source of life from which we all come.

Many women are taught from a young age, directly and indirectly, that the primal workings of their bodies are something to hide and never speak of, unless they are mentioned somewhat disparagingly. Yet these processes are the very fabric of creation, allowing the sacred work of soul union—spirit and body—to happen, allowing all our heavenly parents' children to come into mortality. If Mother God is the archetype of the woman, it makes sense that seeing the sacredness in Her daughters is a precursor to seeing and honoring Her. The generative power in a woman's body—a tree of life in its own right—is the representation of the creative mystery that is the Mother.

Many women face the life-death-life cycle of creation in pregnancy. For many, carrying a child can feel like balancing on the precipice of life and death, waiting for the mysteries of creation working in one's womb to unfold. Within that hidden chamber of the womb, cells speak to cells, and life is either granted, refused, or taken. In that holy of holies, cells become heart cells or lung cells—the Gods brooding over the face of the waters—singing into being, speaking the language of fiber and tissue, of marrow and sinew.

Pregnancy is nine months of unparalleled transformation. More chemical changes occur in a woman's brain during pregnancy than at any other time of her life.[27] The DNA of her male child or children becomes incorporated into hers.[28] Many women leave pregnancy scarred with a range of ongoing complications: hip and spinal misalignments; diastasis recti; tinnitus; receding gum lines; incontinence; joint pain; postpartum depression, anxiety, and obsessive-compulsive disorder (OCD), to name a few. After my first child was born, I experienced postpartum depression that lasted for over a year. In this absence of vitality, I found myself often feeling ambivalent about life and my new child. While I tried to work through the root cause and seek help, I struggled to verbalize my experience to anyone; it felt like an illness of loneliness. Even in my husband's care, there was no way to communicate with him in a way he could understand, as a man who would never birth a child. It felt impossible that many of those I loved continued on without grasping the severity of my condition and were unable to truly ever reach me; mental illness is not something you can see. I did not really know of its severity until I found my way out of its grasp. I am different now. I live with a new capacity for both disconnection and vulnerability, which can be scary and has brought me to greater intimacy with those who have suffered in similar ways.

What it means to carry an unborn child, surrendering oneself in order for someone else to live and breathe, is known only in the female experience. It's impossible to convey the massive alterations that happen during this time of abundance and breaking. Many women connect to the Divine Feminine in this unparalleled way, yet we continue to grapple with how patriarchy has normalized the treatment of women as subordinate, born with inferior abilities. Why the true realm of women goes unacknowledged or often dismissed has everything to do with the creative powers they hold. Across the world, these powers are feared, and we see all too often how this fear leads to control. It is a societal refusal to accept at-one-ment to try and control the bodies of women. Female bodies are served up in the media and marketed as eroticized objects of desire, property for male consumption. In Church culture, the control over women's bodies can look like an inordinate amount of attention paid to asking girls to cover up, focusing on modesty talks to young women, placing the responsibility of men's thoughts on young women, editing middle and high school portraits to cover cleavage and shoulders, and generally viewing women's bodies as ornaments, not instruments.[29] In the face of the understudied creative powers of women, we all have a choice. We can fear or revere the mysterious, we can give space for what we do not understand, or we can belittle it, mock it, fear it, attempt to dominate it, and treat it as "other," outside of our realm of concern.

While pregnancy and childbirth are quintessential in their expressions of the divine ordination of women to creative powers, mothers aren't necessarily privy to a greater understanding of our Mother. As children of Mother God, we are all formed from Her sacred being, and every woman carries the symbolism of the tree of life in her body, whether or not she is a mother on earth. Like any other spiritual knowledge, the specificity of how we, all of heavenly parents' children, come to understand the symbolism of the female body and its unique meaning in the world is dependent on our own personal inquiry and development.

In coming to understand the female body, we all live our unique doctrine that affirms our physicality as divine, capable of sacred union with spirit and mind, from which the wisdom of our heavenly parents emerges and expands our eternal capacities. Our bodies are inherently wise, not inherently sinful. Learning what it is to truly inhabit our bodies and to respect the bodies of others is a major part of our earth-bound quest.

So much possibility for connection comes from making room for the feminine experience in conversation and storytelling, in learning and speaking with reverence about lived experiences. Female wisdom about the cycles of life can inform the way we all live—moving in harmony between periods of productivity and rest, for example—and weave into how we demonstrate reverence for sacred life all around us as we make small and large decisions.

Beautifully, the female body stands for the opposite of hierarchy; it represents networks of healthy systems that are dependent on each other and that cannot exist in isolation or prize one life above another. The female body expresses the beauty, value, and love found in relationality. Understanding its real power and sacred symbolism allows us to love wholly and integrally, to create space for the feminine in our collective healing, which is the same as creating space for the Mother. Changing our discussion about, and portrayals of, the female body to reflect eternal truths communicates to our Mother that we want Her to be a part of our lives and that we want to hear what She has to say.

Our Relationship to Mother Earth

> *Oh what a catastrophe, what a maiming of love when it was made a personal, merely personal feeling, taken away from the rising and setting of the sun, and cut off from the magic connection of the solstice and equinox. This is what is the matter with us. We are bleeding at the roots, because we are cut off from the earth and sun and stars, and love is a grinning mockery, because, poor blossom, we plucked it from its stem on the tree of Life, and expected it to keep on blooming in our civilised vase on the table.*[30]
>
> —D. H. Lawrence

The Eden story is also a story of separation of humankind and the rest of creation. While the scriptures teach us that the Gods intended a binding relationship between humanity and the land—care for it and it will care for you[31]—the fall from the Garden led to the natural world becoming victim to the idea that humankind owns knowledge.[32] In this demarcation is the deeply harmful belief that nature is "other," leading to its objectification, plunder, and commodification. Environmental degradation is directly connected to the devaluation of women, the creators, nurturers, and caretakers of life on earth, and patriarchy's disabling narrative that men have limited responsibility and capacity to be equally nurturing. Deforestation is destroying sacred trees. Living by the rhythms of the seasons and the body has given way to mechanistic production, which does not honor our ecological heritage as humans embedded in creative cycles of growth, harvest, rest, and replenishment. We find ourselves looking back at two thousand years of human-centered Western philosophy that has taught us to retreat into our own heads for solutions to our problems and to prize the rational human mind above nature.

The rationality that was honed in the Enlightenment by Descartes and others is a great tool; it has specific uses and has given us miraculous technological advancement. As effective as it is in its purposes, rationality alone is insufficient because it cannot begin to answer the essential questions of meaning, purpose, and human connection. While raising the standard of living along many metrics for billions, the dominance of rationality has also brought us to what more and more are recognizing as a collective "meaning crisis." We forget, in all our self-referential humanness, that we are creatures of the earth and need to commune with the land. We need grounding, an anchor to place, wherever we live. In our highly secularized world, many have grown to see the physical world as empty of significance, inanimate, or created primarily for human use. In calling the places where we live property, artificially demarcated, we invariably act in ways that are largely ignorant or dismissive of ecological networks that care nothing for our contrived boundaries. And so our environmental crisis derives largely from a disassociation between people and the places they live—a severance that can leave us with feelings of anxiety and despair.[33]

In the Western philosophical tradition, the masculine has often been connected to the qualities of intellect and reason. Intellect and reason have largely been seen as superior to "everything else in nature—everything which is physical, emotional, instinctual and wild," traits shared by nature and the feminine.[34] Because of this, there lingers a societal and cultural perception that both women and nature must never be fully embraced as they are but must be overcome by the uniquely human—masculine—force of reason. In this tradition, men are therefore seen as largely superior to nature and to women.

As the archetype of femininity, Mother God also goes unembraced in this paradigm. We have the opportunity in this life to weave together the good that comes from all types of intelligence—emotional, physical, instinctual, spiritual, as well as rational. And it is primarily in nature where we heed the call of Mother God. Just as we were given divine attributes mirroring our Father before we took on this mortal coil, so were we given attributes emulating our Mother, one being the call of abundance latent inside each of us. There is wisdom only Mother God can give, and it begins to take form in the deep soil of beliefs in our hearts and psyches. As She taught Her son Jesus how to embody feminine intelligence, harmonized with masculine intelligence, Her spirit nurtures our desire for integration and wholeness as we experience Her workings in the land. Earth reveals the divinity of the Mother in its processes, which we can participate in through cultivating the earth and our numerous spiritual and physical gifts. The wisdom of the land, the plants, and the animals is our heritage—the heritage of the Mother.

The connection to the cycles of life manifest in Mother Earth and mirrored in women's bodies is *the* wisdom needed to lessen humanity's collective harm in the world. Mother God reminds us that rootedness to place is rootedness to ourselves, to each other, and to the divine. In the Book of Mormon, we see examples of what it looks like to belong to the earth and to each other. After Jesus's visit to the Nephites and Lamanites, there is a sustained period of time when "there were no contentions and disputations among them, and every man did deal justly one with another. And they had all things common among them; therefore there were not rich and poor, bond and free, but they were all made free, and partakers of the heavenly gift . . . and there still continued to be peace in the land."[35]

Fourth Nephi further defines how "prospering" in the land had everything to do with living in harmony with each other. It is perhaps worth our time to consider how harmony with each other is related to harmony with the land. How would peace among all, in a city or a nation, translate to peace in the forests, rivers, and mountains? A Zion state is linked to a millennial state in scripture: "The wolf and the lamb will feed together, and the lion will eat straw like the ox."[36] "They shall not hurt or destroy in all my holy mountain, for the earth shall be filled with the knowledge of the Lord."[37] Isaiah shows us that godly knowledge, which was given during Jesus's visit to the Nephites and Lamanites, eschews the desire to dominate, ending a reign of hurt and destruction. Godly knowledge leads us to true community, a desire, perhaps, to communicate honestly with each other, to make our relationships go deeper than masks of composure. We live our covenantal commitment to rejoice together and mourn together, to delight in each other, and make others' conditions our own. It's as if we finally believe we deserve abundance, and for all living. We believe in how wholly we are loved and how wholly Earth herself is loved. The knowledge of the Lord is finally understanding the purposes of creation, and I believe that final purpose is love. In that godly wisdom, we can finally surrender in vulnerability together. We can finally answer love's call to give care, attention, recognition, respect, commitment, and trust, as well as honest and open communication—to heed love's transformative power.[38]

The blessings of prosperity then and now continue to belong to those who keep their covenantal commitments, upholding the truth that we are bound together. In Omni 1:6 specifically, "prosper in the land" and "cut off from [the Lord's] presence" are lined up as opposites. This indicates that *prospering in the land* is equivalent to having the Lord's presence.[39] There is something innately divine, then, about living in harmony with the land as well as with our brothers and sisters; it allows for the work of healing and miracles to thrive.[40] These scriptural examples of harmony make me wonder what it would look like, now in our times, to truly belong to each other and the Earth.

On our individual ascension paths, we are called to search for what has been all along: deep presence. If we allow ourselves to be attentive from moment to moment, to our embodied experience, little by little we are taught that we do not live in an abstraction. We do not live in a painting where nature is merely a backdrop but in a world where the divine is infused into every living thing: within our own limbs and hearts, within the food we eat and the soil that makes food possible, within the sun and moon that give light to our eyes.[41] The seemingly paradoxical nature of deity being in and through all things as well as existing in their own bodies of flesh and bone is not, on second thought, paradoxical at all but the very definition of what it means to be divine and to experience the kind of *beingness* that our heavenly parents desire for us.

I remember, when I was seventeen, leaving the house after an argument with my parents. I walked out the front door into the spring drizzle, full of anger and pain, toward the mountains east of Salt Lake City. The air was crisp. Low clouds filled the sky as dusk came on. I walked three miles alone up into the foothills until I reached the canyon. I hiked to an upper trail, hidden by the understory, and lay down in the dirt as the dark settled around me. The earth hummed under my humming body and held me. I let go of my pain and gave it to the mountain. I felt my breathing slow, my gaze soften. The stillness of the night enveloped me. I sensed a deep listening from the spirits of shrub oak and bigtooth maple, a recognition of my presence. I felt, *Your existence is enough. You belong to me, and I to you. Whatever happens will be. The rains will come, or not. What is, is. I am that I am. I am the existing one. You are that you are. You are the existing one.*[42]

The ritual of going out into the natural world in solitude is a vital way to experience deep presence. Our breathing changes. Our attention is restored.[43] We feel rejuvenated, soothed in the rhythms of waves, wind, and birdsong. We encounter the mysterious offerings of attentiveness to creation—epiphany, revelation, transcendence—that have no substitute. By doing so, we commune in ways that allow for the exploration of our internal landscapes, which has the potential to transform our ways of engaging with each other. Richard Rohr, American Franciscan priest and writer, speaks poignantly of the divine revealed by our attentiveness to the outer world and to our inner world: "We come to God through things as they are; spirituality is about sinking back into the Source of everything. We're already there, but we have too little practice seeing ourselves there. God, in Christ, is in all, and through all, and with all."[44]

Learning to listen to the silences, to the great pauses and stillness from moment to moment, may be our greatest quest.

A heightened attention in the world leads naturally to a greater consciousness of our embodiment. In awakening to the reality of our condition—the natural and supernatural contriving—we probe the depths and limits of our knowledge and compassion. We learn that being open to not knowing will bring more knowing. That a state of open-heartedness is necessary for growth and wisdom. As much as we learn about ecosystems, of natural orders and interconnections, there is so much that escapes our understanding and language. So much wonder lies at our feet.

The Mother's influence goes beyond deepening our understanding of our embodiment. We can see the Mother more clearly through Her creations. Mother God can be in plain sight and we miss Her because of the state of our hearts or our distracted minds. She asks for our humility in the face of the other sacred beings She has been instrumental in creating: the ancient wisdom of the redwoods, the language of humpback whales, the touch-mourning of a herd of elephants when one of their own lies down and dies. She asks for the resounding reality of our oneness to be expressed to each other now, in this life. Our own salvation is dependent on loving our neighbor as ourselves. Are the bears, wolves, trees, deer, and sparrows not also our neighbors? If we are doing the inner work of healing and heart expansion, it becomes much easier to see and feel how interdependent we all are, how true it is that our destinies are bound up together.

Profoundly, the Mother also teaches us in our movement toward communion how separate we are from each other in our mortal existence, so that we may have humility in our reaching for interconnection. We are unique beings, yet we are full of forces and energies that can collide and intertwine. Our patterns of relationality and meaning are gathered from the apparently empty spaces between each other as much as they are through our moments of direct communion and connection. She teaches us how we will never fully understand the life of another soul, as tangential as our experiences are. That trying to understand another's experience by imagining ourselves in that experience is not the same as what the other experiences, but that in striving to connect we touch the face of the divine.

Living in the tension of what we know and don't know about others, ourselves, and the Gods is how we grow.

Communion in community is everything to Mother Earth and Mother God. The intelligence inherent in nature's fabric ensures that transformation lies in community. Through our Mother's eyes, we see community as an ever-expanding set of relationships in which our proactive engagement produces ripples of change continuing into the eternities. As She must have taught Her Son, Jesus, how to embody wisdom, unity, and enduring love, Her spirit nurtures our desire for eternal connection as we watch Her workings in the land. An intimate connection to the earth is fundamental to our growth and expansion both temporally and eternally; it is the metamorphosis we need to change Earth's trajectory. Thus, hastening the awakening of the feminine archetype, the cyclical process-oriented pathway to change (rather than the goal-oriented masculine mindset), is the only way to heal Mother Earth and ourselves.

For me, one of the most powerful visions in scripture is of Mother Earth sounding a prophetic voice: "And it came to pass that Enoch looked upon the earth; and he heard a voice from the bowels thereof, saying: Wo, wo is me, the mother of men; I am pained, I am weary, because of the wickedness of my children. When shall I rest, and be cleansed from the filthiness which is gone forth out of me? When will my Creator sanctify me, that I may rest, and righteousness for a season abide upon my face?"[45] She calls out to be saved from the wickedness of her children, to rest in righteousness. She knows she will be saved eventually, but in the agony of the present moment, she calls out for some idea of when she will be free from the destruction and hate that racks her body. She invites us to stay open and vulnerable to her pain. It can seem easier, in our sometimes spiritually infantile approach, to sever a relationship that is in decline—whether from illness or other factors—to leave before the beloved can leave. Earth is a dying beloved, spouse, and mother, and we've severed the relationship because it hurts too much to lose it or because we never truly learned to value it in the first place. Our job now is to fully embrace and embody the reality that the divine is not simply distant beings—it is all of creation. All of creation is the work of divine hands. Every bird, every tree, every soul is a divine revelation.

Is it necessary for our very survival to believe in the sacredness of Mother Earth, that within her is the hidden world of God? How can we possibly know God if we destroy that hidden world? How can we ever know ourselves? For "we cannot protect something we do not love, we cannot love what we do not know, and we cannot know what we do not see. Or hear. Or sense."[46] I believe the denial or acceptance of God begins with how we relate to the world They have created. They did not create it for our personal or collective gain but for our joy, so we may learn that joy is not found in storing up earthly treasures where moth and rust corrupt but in forging eternal bonds.

Mother Earth is an everlasting soul, and unlike ours, her salvation is guaranteed: she will be celestialized. She is our earthly sustenance and security and is promised to be sealed up through the everlasting covenant as an eternal, celestial home. The implications of her innate divinity are staggering;

our own transformation into celestial beings depends on our capacity to envision who she truly is.

Creativity and Godliness

The healing we experience in our cyclical dives into the chambers of our underworld changes us on a cellular level and improves the quality of energy we embody, tuning us to a higher frequency; we experience a greater awareness of what we energetically contain and release into the world. We take greater responsibility for what we radiate. As David O. McKay taught:

> Every man, every person radiates what he or she is. Every person is a recipient of radiation. The Savior was conscious of this fact. Whenever he came into the presence of an individual, he sensed that radiation, whether it was the woman of Samaria with her past life; whether it was the woman who was to be stoned, or the men who were to stone her; whether it was the statesman, Nicodemus, or one of the lepers. Christ was ever conscious of the radiation from the individual, and, to a degree, so are you, and so am I. It is what we are and what we radiate that affects the people around us.[47]

When we are motivated by wisdom and love, our very souls are altered, as is the heart of how we spend our time.

Finding expression in creative forms becomes one of the most direct ways to connect to the divine, including to our Mother. Creative acts are pure manifestations of faith. They are the heartbeat of harmony, pleas for holiness to flow in the land, in our bodies, and through our transformation paths. We weave ideas into new patterns, breathe life into the seemingly lifeless, and live into being stronger and more tender threads of connection. Creative expressions open the mind and spirit to the possibility of transcendent (revelatory) experiences.

As I awoke to the reality of Mother God while carrying my first child, I felt myself moving toward a vast unknown. I was in awe of the new dimension of myself being revealed by pregnancy. What did it mean to be a vessel between the eternal and mortal realms? I marveled at its cosmic and simultaneously intimate reach, as I also felt incredibly daunted by the unknown in a way I never had before. I wanted to understand more profoundly how I resemble my Mother. This time, I recognized divine distancing as a sign of a faith transformation: I was embarking into uncharted territory and realized that a great deal of trust and resolve on my part would be necessary in order to find myself and God again.

I felt what I can only describe as a call compelling me toward the symbolism of the Mother Tree. While my world shifted and a new reality of who I was grew inside me, I turned to poetry, as a way to weave together all I had learned. It was my natural next step to find Her through the influence of poetic composition. I knew that by opening myself to this soul-expanding medium, I would co-create a new depth of perception.

The act of writing each poem remade me. I began to find my voice. I was able to explore the intersection of my own experience of pregnancy and motherhood and my spiritual desires for a feminine landscape within the gospel. There are poems in my collection, *The Tree at the Center,* that were *given* to me. The Mother gave me the words to re-create my soul and, in turn, reflect Her to the world. These poems are as alive and "bright" to me as scripture.[48] I find new connections and meaning with each rereading; they are scripture to me. We all have the spiritual faculties to receive personal revelation that marks our souls as profoundly as any other source of revelation, including canonized scripture. Each kind of recorded and/or received communion has a place in our development. God has told us time and time again that if we ask we will receive.[49] What we receive in answer to this eternal pronouncement and law is illuminated in our hearts and minds: sacred unveilings that re-create our souls.

In a symbolic way, when we create, we participate in states of mind, body, and spirit akin to the Gods who created Earth. In very real ways, we participate in the re-creation of the universe through our individual transformations of intelligence, faith, and presence in the world. Our personal transformations lead ultimately to a shift in collective consciousness, bringing us all closer to wholeness and holiness. I believe this is all in preparation for Her. Our collective movement toward Zion will open the way for Her return.

Taking Stock of Where We Are

What would it be like to have our Mother restored to our most sacred scripts and visionary spaces of the temple? To the Holy of Holies? The archetypal form of womanhood returned so that women may know in whose image they were formed? So that men might see the source of all their feminine wisdom?

What would a healthy, living Mother Tree in our midst mean to the ongoing Restoration?

We will spend the next chapter exploring some of these questions. But first, let's take a moment to look around and see where we are. Before embarking on this journey together, we were on the well-trod masculine path of ascent, a linear trajectory of largely performance-based development in the gospel. We see now that because of its separation from the feminine way the path is troubled with brambles; creeds of patriarchy mar it and obscure our vision. And it is not getting us to the end point. Frankly, it cannot. Traveling down a straight path of masculine understanding, led primarily by law and patriarchal rule with the feminine path nowhere in sight, was not our heavenly parents' intent; Jesus's very life is testament to that. As the Embodied Way, the Completed One, the Union of our Mother and Father, ultimately He points us to Them. And for us in the latter days, at this time in the Restoration, I see Him pointing us to Her. He knows we each need one-on-one time with our Mother.

Our journey in this book focuses on the feminine path, the cyclical, undulating way, tender and new to us like a tiny sapling. Our final goal will be to integrate this new wisdom about the Mother into our lives and understandings. But for now, the path asks for us to stay with it so we may give it the attention it deserves. So we will continue to explore, to let this path grow and mature. In its purity of vision and tenderness, it is more able to reflect us back to ourselves when it is free from obscuring images. It is largely unlabeled with other associations and a long history of men's philosophies, having been exiled for so long. We see more clearly on this path the source of our joy and the source of our pain because the space is still open. As we've seen, an unknown Mother means our vision of ourselves is not healthy. If we, as small and weak saplings in the Mother's image, want to grow, to reach the full stature of our potential, it makes sense that we would speak here first.

In the third part of our journey, "Crown," I hope to sketch a vision of what continuing along the feminine ascension path might look like. We will explore how its full blooming can reveal a feminine side of ourselves that can heal us and mature us and lead to a strong and healthy tree, eventually able to bring us to the marriage of the feminine and masculine that is "the marriage" of the bride to the bridegroom from scripture. This book will not take us to the final union. I, for one, have not yet experienced this oneness and so am entirely unqualified to describe it. Yet I feel incredible hope that we have arrived this far together.

NOTES

1 Wohlleben, *Hidden Life of Trees*, 149.

2 Cynthia Bourgeault, *An Introductory Wisdom School: Course Transcript and Companion Guide* (Wisdom Way of Knowing: 2017), https://wisdomwayofknowing.org/wp-content/uploads/2018/11/Intro-eCourse_Front-Matter_First-Evening_Day-1-Morning.pdf, 3.

3 Doctrine and Covenants 88:6.

4 Jack Kornfield, *A Path with Heart: The Classic Guide through the Perils and Promises of Spiritual Life* (New York: Bantam, 2008), 12.

5 Charles Swift, "Lehi's Archetypal Vision of the Tree of Life," in *The Tree of Life: From Eden to Eternity* (Provo, UT: Neal A. Maxwell Institute for Religious Scholarship, 2011), 137.

6 Rabbi Jill Hammer, "Shekhinah," November 25, 2013, https://rabbijillhammer.com/2013/11/25/shekhinah/.

7 John M. Lundquist, "The Tree of Life in Asian Art, Religion, and Folklore," in *The Tree of Life: From Eden to Eternity* (Provo, UT: Neal A. Maxwell Institute for Religious Scholarship, 2011), 223.

8 Proverbs 8; 2 Chronicles 3:8.

9 Margaret Barker writes, "A key theme in the Qumran Wisdom texts was the *raz nihyeh*, which probably means 'the mystery of existence' or 'the mystery of becoming' that the holy of holies represented. The one who sought Wisdom was exhorted to 'Gaze upon the *raz nihyeh* and know the paths of everything that lives.' Vision was fundamental to Wisdom." See *The Mother of the Lord Volume 1: The Lady in the Temple* (London: Bloomsbury, 2012), 107.

10 2 Kings 22:8.

11 Zina Petersen, "Where Shall Wisdom Be Found?" *Interpreter: A Journal of Latter-day Saint Faith and Scholarship* 7 (2013), 100.

12 Petersen, "Where Shall Wisdom Be Found?" 100.

13 The menorah in the temple was a symbol of the high priesthood and of the high priest's relationship to the Lady. See Barker, *Mother of the Lord*, 65. Elsewhere Barker also asserts that the original menorah in Solomon's Temple may have stood in the Holy of Holies: "The menorah that represented the tree of life was restored to the temple. There had been a menorah in the second temple, as can be seen from the one depicted among the temple loot on the arch of Titus in Rome. Nevertheless, there was a cultural memory that this was not the true menorah: maybe it had stood in the wrong part of the temple, or maybe it no longer represented the tree of life." Barker, http://www.margaret-barker.com/Papers/RestoringSolomon.pdf, 11. According to Barker, "The Lady's great symbol was the tree of life, represented in the old temple by the menorah which originally stood in the holy of holies, the most sacred part of the temple. When John had a vision of the old temple restored, he saw that the tree of life had returned to the holy of holies (Revelation 22.1–5)." Barker, http://www.margaretbarker.com/Papers/TheLadyoftheTempleinaJordanleadbook.pdf.

14 Barker, *Mother of the Lord*, 62.

15 Rabbi Jill Hammer, "Shekhinah."

16 Proverbs 8: 27–28, 30 (Revised Standard Version [RSV]).

17 Proverbs 8:30 (Septuagint [LXX]).

18 Margaret Barker, "Wisdom and the Stewardship of Knowledge," http://www.margaretbarker.com/Papers/WisdomAndTheStewardshipOfKnowledge.pdf. Scriptures suggest that the meaning of *covenant* was connected with creation's order and stability: "Behold I establish my covenant with you and your descendants after you, and with every living creature that is with you . . . the everlasting covenant between God and every living creature of all flesh that is upon the earth" (Genesis 9:9–10, 16). "The earth mourns and withers . . . for they have broken the everlasting covenant" (Isaiah 24:5). Breaking the everlasting covenant, then, would mean destroying the bonds of creation. It would be a rejection of the feminine aspect of deity.

19 Barker, *Mother of the Lord*, 24.

20 Petersen, "Where Shall Wisdom Be Found?" 104.

21 Barker, *Mother of the Lord*, 53.

22 Margaret Barker, "Where Shall Wisdom Be Found?" http://www.margaretbarker.com/Papers/WhereshallWisdombefound.pdf, 2.

23 Proverbs 1:22–28. Margaret Barker translation. See "Where Shall Wisdom Be Found?" 2.

24 Daniel C. Peterson, "Nephi and His Asherah," *Journal of Book of Mormon Studies* 9, no. 2 (2000), https://scholarsarchive.byu.edu/jbms/vol9/iss2/4.

25 Mosiah 8:20.

26 I go into more detail later in the book about what is missing in the temple space.

27 Chelsea Conaboy, "Motherhood Brings the Most Dramatic Brain Changes of a Woman's Life," *Globe Magazine*, July 17, 2018, https://www.bostonglobe.com/magazine/2018/07/17/pregnant-women-care-ignores-one-most-profound-changes-new-mom-faces/CF5wyPob5EGCcZ8fzLUWbP/story.html.

28 William F. N. Chan, Cécile Gurnot, Thomas J. Montine, Joshua A. Sonnen, Katherine A. Guthrie, and J. Lee Nelson, "Male Microchimerism in the Human Female Brain," *PLOS ONE* 7, no. 9 (September 26, 2012), https://journals.plos.org/plosone/article?id=10.1371/journal.pone.0045592.

29 See Dr. Lexie Kite and Dr. Lindsay Kite, *More Than a Body: Your Body Is an Instrument, Not an Ornament* (Boston: Mariner Books, 2020).

30 From *Lady Chatterley's Lover*.

31 The Everlasting Covenant was a covenant between El Shaddai (male and female deity, like the *'elohim* of Genesis 1:26) and all of creation, made first to Adam and renewed through Enoch, Noah, and Abraham. See Exodus 6:3–4; Genesis 9:9–10, 16.

32 Barker, "Wisdom and the Stewardship of Knowledge," 8.

33 There are many articles and studies available on what is termed "eco-anxiety." Here is a link to a recent article: https://www.medicalnewstoday.com/articles/327354. Excerpt: "Researchers coined the term 'eco-anxiety' to describe chronic or severe anxiety related to humans' relationship with the environment. In 2017, the American Psychiatric Association (APA) described eco-anxiety as 'a chronic fear of environmental doom.'"

34 Blackie, *If Women Rose Rooted*, 33.

35 4 Nephi 1:2–4.

36 Isaiah 65:25 (New International Version [NIV]).

37 Isaiah 11:9.

38 M. Scott Peck beautifully defines love as such in his book *The Road Less Traveled.*

39 Book of Mormon Central Team, "What Does It Mean to 'Prosper in the Land'?" June 7, 2016, https://knowhy.bookofmormoncentral.org/knowhy/what-does-it-mean-to-prosper-in-the-land.

40 4 Nephi 1:5.

41 Doctrine and Covenants 88:6–13.

42 A common translation of the Hebrew phrase הֶיְהֶא רֶשָׁא הֶיְהֶא, 'ehyeh 'ăšer 'ehyeh ([ʔehˈje ʔaˈʃer ʔehˈje]), is "I am that I am," along with "I am who I am," "I will become what I choose to become," "I am what I am," "I will be what I will be," "I create what(ever) I create," or "I am the Existing One." https://www.jstor.org/stable/pdf/1515709.pdf?refreqid=excelsior%3Ae52a69d8a4970832bd40f514644af906.

43 Spending time in nature has many benefits, including reduced anxiety and stress, increased attention capacity and creativity, and an ability to engage and connect with others. See Jill Suttie, "How Nature Can Make You Kinder, Happier, and More Creative," *Greater Good Magazine*, March 2, 2016, https://greatergood.berkeley.edu/article/item/how_nature_makes_you_kinder_happier_more_creative.

44 Richard Rohr, "All Creation Has Soul," Center for Action and Contemplation, February 14, 2021, https://cac.org/all-creation-has-soul-2021-02-14/.

45 Moses 7:48.

46 Richard Louv, *The Nature Principle: Human Restoration and the End of Nature-Deficit Disorder* (Chapel Hill, NC: Algonquin Books of Chapel Hill), 104.

47 Address of David O. McKay for the 139th Conference of The Church of Jesus Christ of Latter-day Saints, April 6, 1969, in 1969 Conference Reports of The Church of Jesus Christ of Latter-day Saints, 150–53, made available by Education and Leadership Foundations, David O. McKay School of Education at Brigham Young University, https://www.education.byu.edu/mckay/69APR6.html.

48 Alma 37:5.

49 Matthew 7:7.

CHAPTER THREE

Crown

Heavens: Above All Things

The crown encompasses all the branches, blossoms, leaves, and fruit of the tree. Just as does the trunk, grown sturdy as it draws strength from the roots, the branches and stems play the role of structural support for the tree's leaves, fruits, and flowers. Branches are the vessels that carry water from the soil to the leaves, and food from the leaves to the rest of the tree. Leaves transform light into sugar, releasing oxygen into the air. They also filter dust and protect the soil below from excessive erosion from rainfall.

The tree puts an incredible amount of resources and energy into seed production; it is a design used by trees for millennia to ensure the next generation exists. A seed, a ripened ovule, houses an embryo, the new plant, and nourishes and protects it. Inside each seed are all the resources needed to survive independently until it reaches a safe place to grow. It contains all the information necessary to produce a new plant.

Usually, a tree grows its branches until the crown encounters neighboring trees of the same height. Its branches stop growing instead of entering the others' space, creating separation lines and boundaries in the sky. Rather than encroach, the tree finds greater benefit from coexistence.[1] Trees have a sophisticated system for measuring light and telling time. They can tell whether light is coming from the sun or being reflected off leaves. When they discern that light is being reflected off leaves, they know there's another plant nearby and that they need to slow down growth in that direction. It's also a way for trees to optimize light exposure for everything under the canopy.

Above all things, our Mother Tree is love expanding outside of time. Her reach is endless. Her branches extend out into the world, responsive to seasonal changes, elemental shifts, and to all of Her children. She knows how they need to grow. In the crown of the tree, we begin to see as our Mother sees;[2] we walk in the way of discernment.[3] In all the regions of the Mother Tree, we are taught how to distinguish truth from falsehoods, reality from delusions, and to embrace that which binds through love.

We heed the Mother's voice in our hearts that says we are one.

As we learn to trust Her more, we in turn open ourselves to greater visions of what is real and lasting. "Farther up is further in."[4] We descend lower and lower and ascend higher and higher to continue to discover both ourselves and Her. In this process of remaking ourselves time and time again, we sink deeper into our own humanity and ascend higher into our divinity—the one embracing the other. We learn the holy power of the interconnectedness of all things past, present, and future. As we've seen, Her wisdom moves us to consider life at macro and cosmic levels.

The Center

The tree of life not only reflects the endless regeneration of the cosmos and thereby its design of efflorescence, but it also offers a sacred lens through which we can apprehend our relation to time. The tree is our key to divine time. It is the undying center of the cosmos where we are rooted to the past, the present, and the future. The tree is our key to divine subjectivity, too. It is the outward manifestation of the inner world of God, "for, just as the seed contains the tree, and the tree the seed, so the hidden world of God contains all Creation, and Creation is, in turn, a revelation of the hidden world of God."[5]

This more mystical approach to understanding God may seem foreign, yet we have been taught countless times to approach God through our own mystic tradition. We are taught to ponder and meditate in order to commune with God. By mysticism I mean our belief that a direct connection can be made with God through inner stillness—cultivated by sitting and thinking—through opening ourselves to questions and the Spirit. Often understood in Christian tradition as coming to union with God, mysticism is the belief that some form of contact with the divine or transcendent is possible. Medieval and early modern Jewish literature reveal the tree of life as an expression of the mystical, rooted in the otherworldly, and knowable only through revelation that moves individuals into a place of communion with the infinite. Our own tree of life vision in the Book of Mormon maps the same journey to our spiritual center and connecting point with deity at the tree. The emphasis in Lehi's dream was on the glowing fruit of the tree's crown, the apex of our desire for God and of God's desire for us.

The Book of Mormon begins with pointing us back to the sacred tree that existed from all eternity and shows the embodied love of God as the endpoint of our spiritual journey.

The tree of life is the mystic center, the point of absolute beginning, and it is the point to which we seek to return. As such, it is the ultimate source of reality, the one cosmic point from which we can orient correctly. Like those on the path in Lehi's vision, we move toward Her. She is the magnetic point of our attention, toward whom we are either repelled or compelled. Her central, cosmic form reveals our hearts to ourselves.

Philosopher of religion Mircea Eliade, one of the world's foremost interpreters of religious symbolism and myth, gives us insight:

> The center . . . is pre-eminently the zone of the sacred, the zone of absolute reality. Similarly, all the other symbols of absolute reality (trees of life and immortality, Fountain of Youth, etc.) are also situated at the center. . . . The road [leading to the center] is arduous, fraught with perils, because it is, in fact, a rite of the passage from the profane to the sacred, from the ephemeral and illusory to reality and eternity, from death to life, from [human] to the divinity. Attaining the center is equivalent to a consecration, and initiation; yesterday's profane and illusory existence gives place to a new, to a life that is real, enduring, and effective.[6]

Gazing upward into Her brilliant boughs, we realize that our willingness to see things as they really are[7] is our gateway to greater wisdom. She endows us with eyes that can see and ears that can hear, for "she is glimpsed at the very edge of our perception and heard among familiar words which seem to tell a different tale. Wisdom is only discerned by those who have Wisdom, because her first gift is the gift of herself."[8] We seek our Mother, Lady Wisdom, and desire that She would rule over us.[9] Like our Mother—She who knows everything that lives by name—we're ready to expand our understanding into the creative mysteries.

As we've seen, in ancient Israel's wisdom tradition, the tree of life appears as a personification or symbolic representation of wisdom. Barker offers this insight: "Wisdom, by means of the images used to depict her, addresses such questions as the relationship between the human and the divine, the means of apotheosis, the stewardship of knowledge, and the power which knowledge gives to transform or to destroy."[10] The Book of Wisdom (also known as The Wisdom of Solomon) is an exhortation to pursue Wisdom as the guide to the kingdom of God. It is one of the seven Sapiential, or wisdom, books in the Septuagint, the others being Psalms, Proverbs, Ecclesiastes, Song of Songs (Song of Solomon), Job, and Sirach. It is included in the deuterocanonical books of the Catholic Church and the *anagignoskomena* of the Eastern Orthodox Church, while most Protestants consider it part of the Apocrypha. The Book of Wisdom reveals Wisdom's true nature:

> Wisdom is radiant and unfading,
> and she is easily discerned by those who love her,
> and is found by those who seek her.
> She hastens to make herself known to those who desire her.
> One who rises early to seek her will have no difficulty,

for she will be found sitting at the gate.
To fix one's thought on her is perfect understanding,
and one who is vigilant on her account will soon be free
from care,
because she goes about seeking those worthy of her,
and she graciously appears to them in their paths,
and meets them in every thought.
The beginning of Wisdom is the most sincere desire for
instruction,
and concern for instruction is love of her,
and love of her is the keeping of her laws,
and giving heed to her laws is assurance of immortality,
and immortality brings one near to God;
so the desire for Wisdom leads to a kingdom.[11]

These verses remind me of James 1:5: "If any of you lacks wisdom, you should ask God, who gives generously to all without finding fault, and it will be given to you."[12] Lady Wisdom, as is true of Jesus and the Father, is only as far from us as we make Her. If we seek Her, She will be found in the center of our hearts and the center of heaven. If we sincerely desire Her divine instruction, She will give it. If we love Wisdom—the way of becoming—She will make Herself known.[13]

Oil of Wisdom

In the temple and tabernacle spaces of the Old Testament, the mystic center of worship and ritual, finding the Mother there was literally a sacred consecration. The high priest was anointed by an oil that made him the child of Wisdom and the son of God. Wisdom is described as the oil itself: a sweet perfume of myrrh, cinnamon, and olive oil.[14] It is also described in Exodus in the instructions for the tabernacle.[15] As Barker describes, "The perfumed anointing oil was kept in the holy of holies, and when the royal high priest was anointed, he received the gift of Wisdom herself: resurrection, life, vision, knowledge and true wealth. The high priest was anointed on his head and between his eyelids . . . which must have symbolised the opening of his eyes."[16]

When the temple oil was hidden in the time of Josiah's purges, to keep it safe from abuse, Enoch described the priests losing their vision.[17] The idea of wisdom being gifted in fragrant oil appears in various texts from the early Christian period. In the *Clementine Recognitions*, Clement ascribes to Peter this elucidation of the word *Christ:* "The Son of God, the Beginning of all things, became Man. He was the first whom God anointed with oil taken from the wood of the tree of life."[18] Peter said Jesus the Christ would anoint those who entered the kingdom. According to this record, the original anointing oil came from the tree of life in the Garden. Peter considered all other oils used in ritual anointings to be copies, as they were not from the tree of life, whose oil was considered most powerful. Peter continues, "Aaron the first high priest was anointed with a composition of chrism which was made after the pattern of the spiritual ointment," and if this earthly copy was so powerful, how much greater was the oil from a branch of the tree of life?[19] In 2 Corinthians, Paul writes to the Corinthians about "the fragrance of the knowledge of Christ . . . a fragrance from life to life"[20]—a fragrance from the tree of life that leads to life eternal.

Aromas and fragrances evoke visceral responses to associated memories and feelings. It's incredibly tender to me that our Mother would speak to us of the visions of the eternal realm through Her very sensuous presence, ultimately transforming us into Her children, children of Lady Wisdom. In Her very lifeblood is a remembering of who we really are and where we really come from. Her sacred oil sparks vision.

The Tree of Imagination

> *The term "imaginal realm" . . . is more an archetype than an idea. . . . It separates the visible world from realms invisible but still perceivable through the eye of the heart. In fact, this is what the word "imagination" specifically implies in its original Islamic context: direct perception through this inner eye, not mental reflection or fantasy. The imaginal penetrates this denser world in much the same way as the fragrance of perfume penetrates an entire room, subtly enlivening and harmonizing.*[21]
>
> —Cynthia Bourgeault

Islamic mystics recognized a real plane of imagination and called it the *'al-mithal*, the world of image, or the *'alam-i-malakut*, the world of imagination. They believed it to be "an intermediary realm, existing between, and interpenetrating the realms of intellect and sense perception,"[22] a plane between the physical, material world and the spiritual world. According to this definition, imagination is the central means of the soul by which the senses and intellect, mind and body, spirit and matter, are able to interrelate.

The need to connect one's purpose and identity through the thread of imagination to the outside world, in order to describe and make sense of reality, is universal. By imaginary I do not mean pretend, but as Cynthia Bourgeault describes in the epigraph, a special way of seeing, a different but real plane of experience. This plane, termed "visionary" in our world, is most often associated with illusory or subjective realms of internal perceptions that carry little weight in our highly secularized and scientific world. Our increasing dependence on technological advances and empirical evidence seems to render this type of seeing secondary, leaving us disconnected from a fundamental mode of understanding, a lost art of perception and memory.

> *"Like the Tree, imagination is the source of endless regeneration."*[23]

The tree of imagination is the structure of imagination itself. Like the tree, imagination serves to unite heaven and earth. Its branches and accompanying fruit represent "the fact that a single archetypal image . . . can produce throughout space and time such an abundant flowering and branching of images."[24] Thoughts germinate like seeds, rise in the nourishment of wisdom and light-intelligence, feeding root and stem to bear fruit that will, in turn, produce more creative beginnings.

The tree of imagination is not stationary or fixed. It continues to evolve and represents a reimagining of our origin and destiny. Being both old and young, with autumns and springs, it discards old meanings and creeds and enables us to shed and dress the tree in eternal truths, to discard archaic imagery and more fully and actively participate in the present.

I am discovering, as poet Jorie Graham describes, that "imagination is a bodily sense. Imagination is not an intellectual capacity."[25] We are here to experience the full measure of embodiment, and yet our reality has been thinned down by our technology. Images and ideas are now relegated to "data"—they used to be more sensorially connected. We rely now almost entirely on visual information and calculation or measurement. What does it mean to embody truth, rather than simply read or hear information? How do we incorporate light and truth? Can the Mother—found in every moment we strive for integration of heart, mind, and body—along with the Spirit and our covenantal commitments, call us to daily practices of communion with the actual, material world? Can the fragrance of Her presence awaken us to our shared memory of Wisdom, gained before this mortal life, including the interconnections that literally make us who we are? To come back into the wisdom of embodiment, we have to uncollapse our lives from the superficial present to which they have been reduced in our information age. Returning to the sounds and senses of the natural world, not images or ideas alone, awakens our capacity to feel what is lasting and to love it, desperately.

This kind of imagination brings us to Wisdom.

We enter the final portion of our journey together holding questions sparked in the imaginal realm: How do we show up in the world after we have tasted who the Mother is? What does it look like to live into the reality of Mother God expressed in you? What would it be like to have Her return to the core of our teachings? Let us consider two examples of how summoning the imaginal realm leads to real fruit: the first from the Book of Alma, and the second from the Gospel of Mary. Each not only reveals the paramount and central role of the tree in the psyche of ancient prophets and peoples but also illustrates the individual struggle and determination necessary to arise and awake through all the vulnerabilities of love.

Alma's Imaginal Tree of Life

The prophet Alma uses the tree as an ascension image to describe an inward journey of spiritual transformation.[26] The seed, planted in the heart, is compared to the utterances of God. If accepted in the heart, the inward phenomenon of nourishing the word-seed brings life exponentially—branches spring up into everlasting life—a brilliant expansion of spirit, heart, and mind.

For the seed of our tree to take root, we must "exercise a particle of faith," meaning that we need only the desire to believe.[27] I take this to mean two important things. First, the power of our agency begins with our summoning of the imaginal realm. We can relate the process to the notion presented in our temple ritual: every living soul was first imagined, sketched before entering the earthly realm. Second, faith is what we form. Faith is choosing to act rather than to be acted upon. As Alma teaches, is it not a complete knowledge but our chosen relationship with the world. Like the Mother Tree, we adapt, bend, and respond to each moment with our whole souls. Faith is the ecstatic space between the realized and the yet to be.

The path to deity, to becoming, is as much a path toward the numinous as it is a path toward enlightenment—two sides of the same whole. As we make more connections and embody more understanding, we simultaneously become more aware of the vastness of what is unknown to us. It is a continuous weaving. Alma teaches that it is our destiny to grow in abundance, to flow in this river of intuition. So the fruit we produce may satisfy. It is the imagining, an eye of faith in so many potentialities, that allows for our hearts to expand into the reality of our material and spiritual substance—to alchemize new understanding into cellular change.

Becoming a constant gardener of our internal tree requires a love for who we are and where we are in the present moment. We remain fully open to the possibility of what we can't yet see—the tree growing—realizing truth is responsive and keeps us in motion. We pray ceaselessly.[28]

As Alma teaches, "Because ye have tried the experiment, and planted the seed, and it swelleth and sprouteth, and beginneth to grow, ye must needs know that the seed is good."[29] We reach a point where there is no longer a question as to the goodness and rightness of the tree, of its ability to survive and thrive, or of our ability to care for it; we are the tree. Through the tending and nurturing of the tree, we have tended to and nurtured ourselves, expanding our capacity for oneness and surrender, confirming our allegiance to life, and rejecting messengers of darkness and destruction.

What fascinates me the most about Alma's description of the mature soul-tree is that its fruit is available to us in this life: "And because of your diligence and your faith and your patience with the word in nourishing it, that it may take root in you, behold, by and by ye shall pluck the fruit thereof, which is most precious, which is sweet above all that is sweet, and which is white above all that is white, yea, and pure above all that is pure; and ye shall feast upon this fruit even until ye are filled, that ye hunger not, neither shall ye thirst."[30] Making room in our hearts for Wisdom to nurture our roots and strengthen our limbs, we see the planes of the sacred and profane merging: heaven is now. As Elder Neal A. Maxwell has put it so beautifully, "We need to concentrate on what has been called 'the holy presence,' for now is sacred. . . . The holy gift of life always takes the form of now."[31]

We find a strikingly similar description of spiritual ascent in the lesser-known extracanonical texts the Gospel of Mary of Magdalene and the Gospel of the Beloved Companion. Here, Mary also relates a vision of the inner journey and reveals more about the final manifestation of all our efforts.

Mary's Imaginal Tree of Life

In the gnostic Gospel of Mary of Magdala, Mary Magdalene shares a vision with the twelve disciples after Christ's resurrection. It is an ascension vision in which she meets and surpasses seven demons on her way to self-actualization. Each demon claims that Mary belongs to the world below and to them, the Powers who control it. In each dialogue between Mary and the Powers, it becomes clear that their domination is founded on lies, their ignorance of God, and their lust for power. She turns away from each in succession: darkness, desire, ignorance, zeal for death, realm of the flesh, false peace, and wrath.[32]

In another version of Mary's vision, from the Gospel of the Beloved Companion, Mary's soul journey is symbolized as an ascent through the boughs of a tree. The tree consists of seven layers or levels of boughs. Before she may ascend into each subsequent level, she must eat the associated fruit. As she climbs, she eats the fruit of love and compassion, wisdom and understanding, honor and humility, strength and courage, clarity and truth, power and healing, and light and goodness. She is allowed to receive the fruit only after she passes the gatekeeper who guards it. These gatekeepers challenge those who try to pass.

After eating the seventh fruit, she ascends to the crown of the tree where she receives Grace and Beauty. And then she sees an arresting figure: "In the light, I beheld a woman of extraordinary beauty, clothed in garments of brilliant white. The figure extended its arms, and I felt my soul drawn into its embrace, and in that moment I was freed from the world, and I realized that the fetter of forgetfulness was temporary."[33] Then the voice of Jesus tells her that she has become the "completion of completions" or the "completeness of I Am," having known the truth of herself.[34]

We know seven is a number of significance. According to the creation texts of Judaism, Christianity, and Islam, it is the number of days the Gods needed to create Earth. In many traditions it is associated with apotheosis, or divinization. That Mary Magdalene overcame seven devils is seen by most of Christianity as a remarkable and rare transformation. Elder Bruce R. McConkie writes, "Hers was no ordinary illness, and we cannot do other than to suppose that she underwent some great spiritual test—a personal Gethsemane, a personal temptation in the wilderness for forty days, as it were—which she overcame and rose above—all preparatory to the great mission and work she was destined to perform."[35]

These accounts of imaginal trees of life from scripture add incredible depth to the idea that we carry the kingdom inside us.[36] Our celestial home is not only a future, glorified Earth; "heaven is . . . a state into which we are invited now."[37]

Eternity is now.

We see the divine and sacred woven throughout all of creation. We move closer to seeing as the Gods, with "all present before our eyes."[38] We fulfill prophecy: "And it shall come to pass in the last days, saith God, I will pour out of my Spirit upon all flesh: and your sons and your daughters shall prophesy, and your young men shall see visions, and your old men shall dream dreams."[39] We trust our imaginations. In this sense we are beginning to rise above all things. We become free from the desires of a telestial realm.

Communion and Consciousness

Is sorrow the true wild?
And if it is—and if we join them—your wild to mine—
what's that?
For joining, too, is a kind of annihilation.
What if we joined our sorrows, I'm saying.
I'm saying: What if that is joy?[40]

—Ross Gay

She is the recognition of sorrow as the true wild. Our Mother Tree teaches us that sorrow, fear, loss, death, dissolution, and decay make joy, love, connection, and rebirth possible. She teaches us how to go to the grief and to not turn our back on it. She teaches us that our imagination catalyzes compassion. Our ability to bridge our intellectual and sensorial experiences of life into an empathetic imagining of another's sorrow binds us together in tender acknowledgment and reverence. We surrender to heartbreak, knowing that it is in sorrow with someone else that we truly learn what is worth living for. In love for all that is tender inside ourselves and the world, we find that life and death are two hands folded together. She is with us as we learn how sorrow sustains and roots us to ourselves. She asks for us to feel past all our intellectual work of making the world into a series of symbols, to just be in presence with the sentient beings all around. She knows that in this sacred space of consciousness with all creation, we will find integrity. And through integrity, communion. She sets us on the path toward the profound and saving compassion that Jesus perfectly embodies.

Through the whisperings of Lady Wisdom, I have come to see enlightenment as intimacy with all things. My covenantal commitment to mourn with those who mourn and to comfort those who stand in need of comfort is the only path to illumination and, thus, joy. For it is only in going to the place of sorrow with those who are sorrowing that I can truly mourn *with*. It is a joining of sorrows, a weaving of roots, a tender turning to each other that bears the fruit of love. Seeing ourselves in each other, my sorrow as your sorrow, yours as mine, is love. And in that love is the only joy. This kind of joining is the only path to knowing Mother and Father God. And that knowing is life eternal. That knowing is joy.

With all that the tree symbolizes—immortality, the divine center and source of life, sustenance of life, life everlasting, wisdom, the abode of the gods, the ascension of the soul—we learn what it means to uncover our true identities, to be healed and whole, sovereign children of the Divine Father and the Divine Mother. Access to this path of healing is offered to us through the grace of Christ's atonement, which is the result of the fully integrated love and power of the feminine and masculine powers of creation and being.

As children of God, it is in our nature to seek soul work and communion. The essence of goodness inside each of us yearns for the wisdom of our Mother, for unity and love, because we know intuitively, instinctually, that we are nothing alone. Without love we are nothing. Without connection we are unable to feel. It is only through *others* that we learn patience, sorrow, anger, frustration, and regret. As hooks states, "When we choose to love we choose to move against fear—against alienation and separation. The choice to love is a choice to connect—to find ourselves in the other."[41]

The Mother teaches me that love is *the* fabric of creation, the only true power and authority. I feel this truth reverberate inside me, and I consider creation made of the same love that literally runs through each of us. At times we may wonder, as Alfred Lord Tennyson did, if nature is nothing but "red in tooth and claw,"[42] unfeeling and indifferent to our existence, not to mention our hopes and dreams. It is my belief that love runs through the workings of creation as a law, even if we, like Job, are unable to see it or comprehend its purposes. In a fallen world, it may be even harder to fathom. The great energy force inside of all creation, because it is the creation of God, drives toward eternal purposes, love, balance, and compassion. Living this truth, in our bodies, is the greatest gift we can give each other and the world. It is the greatest expression of charity. It is the final expression of charity. If we master it individually and collectively, it will bring us to Zion and will return us all, in the bond of the covenant of peace, back to our heavenly home.

Your tree of life grows inside you, manifesting your eternal soul to yourself. Manifesting the divine inside yourself—a vision of the cosmos. You are a vision of the cosmos.

The Ascension Path, an Upward Spiral

> *Terms like "ground" and "source" stand in contrast to the terms used for the transcendent biblical God of history who is known as a supreme king, a father, a creator, a judge, a maker. When he creates the world, he does so as do males, producing something external to himself. He remains essentially outside of and judges the creative processes he has initiated. As ground and source, God creates as does a mother, in and through her own very substance. As ground of being, God participates in all the joys and sorrows of the drama of creation which is, at the same time, the deepest expression of the divine life. God's unchanging unitary life and that of the cosmos' ever-changing, dynamic multiplicity ultimately reflect a single unitary reality.*[43]
>
> —Richard L. Rubenstein

Like the structure of a tree's canopy, in Mother God's pattern of spiritual growth is repetition with variety: we are repeatedly asked to break our hearts open so that they may grow and accept more and more love, though each specific way we come to that breaking point changes over the course of our lives. Feminine wisdom interweaves the necessity for cyclical ascents and descents into the realm of the roots with the more masculine movement of linear progression. United, they create an upward spiral of transformation. If we picture in our minds a tree in profile, we can see the repetition of the tree's layered branches mimicking the shape of an upward spiral, while the trunk forms a straight vertical line. We see another iteration of the united feminine and masculine aspects in the rod and serpent motif. The feminine is symbolized as the undulating, sensual form of the snake wrapped around the straight line of the rod, the masculine aspect. This is an image of health, wholeness, and power to this day.[44]

In contrast, we see many attempting a purely upward trajectory, demarcated by performative markers. This futile path, described in scripture as "ever learning, and never able to come to the knowledge of the truth,"[45] is exemplified by the Pharisees of the New Testament and in the story of the Tower of Babel. Those invested in the tower tried, as many have, to get to heaven without doing the radical (and radial) soul work required. They attempted to build an outward manifestation of what they should have been cultivating inside: communion with God. Thinking they could climb to heaven, they rejected their own transformation path, their hearts, and God Themselves in the process.

As expressed in the conceptualization of yin and yang, the feminine and masculine reside inside each of us.[46] As children of divine parents, we each hold within ourselves the potential of a full realization of feminine and masculine qualities. And because we are all unique individuals, unique expressions are expected. There isn't a prescribed way to manifest these parts of us or the expectation that we must relate with all iterations on an infinite spectrum. Part of coming to know deity (and ourselves) is being able to sift out what true femininity and true masculinity are for us as opposed to traditions or cultural constructs. It takes a balance of perspectives and gifts to fully actualize our potential. It requires that the masculine awakes from the slumber of the Garden and remembers wholeness is not without the feminine, and that the feminine in turn learns to recognize and trust healthy expressions of the masculine. It is a never-ending journey toward a more integral form of self that develops sovereignty and true power, anchored in generosity.

Just as the fruit of the tree of knowledge of good and evil was insufficient to save Eve and Adam, the knowledge alone of good and evil in our lives is not enough to save us. All the sets of dualities of the tree of knowledge transform by purpose and love through the tree of life, the tree of wisdom. Described by Nephi as the fruit of the tree of life, the offspring of the Mother, Jesus is reborn through His reconciliation of the disparities of this world. We, in turning to the tree of life, awaken to the reality that we must also become the reconciliation. It is our destiny also to become whole through the tree of life.

As we see so perfectly manifest in Jesus, in His balancing of the feminine and masculine principles of spiritual growth, it is impossible to have unity with ourselves and God without submitting to the mysteries of God's hidden world. It feels more than possible that Mother God taught Her son, Jesus, how to contain multitudes.[47] Multitudes of souls, identities, ideas, and perspectives—all the shades of darkness and light necessary to embody every living soul and so then be empowered to know the world wholly. In this knowing is the power to harmonize the world, to grow Her children, to push them to the edge of their knowledge and then teach them how to weave new patterns: how to co-create the world anew alongside the Gods.

Real faith ruptures boundaries.

Finding our individual balance of the feminine and masculine wisdom that our Heavenly Mother and Heavenly Father have allows for our souls' rest. Now. In this life.

Divine Rest in the Fragrant Tree

> *When our rising love and joyful gratitude meet the shower of mercy and love from the Savior and from our heavenly parents, in that contact is the pure radiance and the brilliant light of glory.*[48]
>
> —Chieko Okazaki

On Enoch's visionary journey in heaven, recorded in the Book of Enoch, he saw a great tree by the throne, "whose fragrance was beyond all fragrance, and whose leaves and blossoms and wood never wither or rot."[49] As Barker describes, "No mortal could touch the tree until after the great judgement, when its fruit would be given to the chosen ones, and the tree itself transplanted again into the temple."[50] The fruit of the tree is compared to the clusters on a palm or to grapes. The most stunning image to me is in Enoch's revelation that the tree is the place where the Lord rests when He is in Paradise: "I saw Paradise, and in the midst, the tree of life, at that place where the Lord takes his rest when he goes (up) to Paradise."[51]

Even the Father finds rest with the Mother Tree.

As we find described in scripture, including the Book of Mormon, the tree is more pleasant, fragrant, and beautiful than any other created thing: "Its appearance is gold and crimson and with the form of fire."[52] In an account of the life of Eve and Adam written at the end of the Second Temple period, when God returns to Paradise, the chariot throne rests at the tree of life, and all its flowers bloom.[53]

The tree is shown as inseparable from the throne. The synagogue at Dura-Europos depicts a king enthroned in a tree. The Letter of Barnabas says that the royal kingdom of Jesus is founded on a tree.[54] In the Book of Revelation, faithful Christians are promised that they will eat the fruit of the tree of life,[55] which stands by the throne of God-and-the-Lamb, watered by the river of life.[56]

Nephi was right: the Mother Tree is love. Love that is piercing, all-knowing, unapologetic, painful, expansive, omnipresent, all-powerful, and binding. The laws of the universe and the laws of the soul. The wisdom of healthy boundaries and intuition, adjusting for circumstances and the ever-changing dynamics of the pulsing and breathing and never-static realms of the universe. She opens our eyes and loosens our tongues so that we become Her children, able to prophesy and testify, able to stand as witnesses of Her unifying and healing powers in the last days. In Her boughs the Father rests. In Her boughs the Son continues to be nurtured. In Her boughs the Son waits for us to partake of Him. We also can find true rest in Her true embrace.

Sacred Groves

Theologies formed by argumentation and creed largely dominate the religious world and minimize the reality of other ways of arriving at knowledge, of understanding and creating meaning. They often discount the necessary place of the ineffable in knowledge creation, the power of the unknown and unknowable. The spaces in between. The Mother honors women as theologians claiming knowledge from their own bodies, knowledge that is not always translatable and that may actually become degraded when relegated to language for consumption in the world. New considerations in theological discourse surrounding the feminine are paramount to our collective survival and salvation, not to mention the very vitality of our religious discourse.

The harmonizing of feminine and masculine principles inside our souls leads to an internal Zion-scape, one that begs reconsideration of the supremacy of the rational over the emotional, the linear over the cyclical, and the quantifiable over the experiential. It asks that we recognize how privileging the masculine above the feminine bears bad fruit, and considers a more inclusionary approach.

Greater sovereignty in our spiritual journeys teaches that there is not just one Sacred Grove but that there are groves everywhere, and you and I can and must enter as part of the rolling out of light and truth, the expansion of the ongoing Restoration. The Mother is also our guide into the heart of our groves. She is here to teach us obscured portions of the ascension path, to round out our theology of argumentation and creed with the theology of the body, a theology of the ineffable, the mysterious, the symbolic, the cellular song, the intuitive knowing so beautifully expressed in Her Son, Jesus the Christ. She confirms His teachings that there is no domination in God.

She is the veil parted, the signs given, our spiritual eyes open, our tongues loosed with the gift of prophecy. "She is a tree of life to those who take hold of her; those who hold her fast will be blessed."[57] I await the return of Lady Wisdom and see many engaged in preparing a way for Her to usher in an order and peace that weaves together all knowledge and truth in one great Restoration.

I imagine Mother God, the Mother Tree returned from exile—our inner landscapes unburdened by the blindness of mortality, our attachment to power surrendered, and Earth finally at rest. I envision a world anointed by Her dew—Her love—and hope quickens my heart.

Cube of Fire*

And maybe we have to consider
that if we find the fluttering heat
of maternal wings missing,
the cube of fire, the heart of creation now
a place of darkness, where

love outside time and every dancing figure
of Ezekiel's Living Ones
have passed,

that She, once in the midst of everything,
like the subtlest, sweetest fragrance of home,
must be restored. And who

are these temple priests
slated to return—the shadow of exile
dusting their trailing robes,
palm leaves in hand—if not you,
if not me?[58]

**The Cube of Fire, a twenty-cubit cube lined with gold, was the Holy of Holies in the Jerusalem temple and the residence of the Mother of the Lord (1 Kings 6:20). It represented the origin and heart of creation.*

1 Crown shyness is a phenomenon that occurs in some tree species when spaces appear in the canopy to prevent branches from touching, forming channel-like gaps. See Katherine J. Wu, "Some Trees May 'Social Distance' to Avoid Disease," *National Geographic*, July 6, 2020, https://www.nationalgeographic.com/science/article/tree-crown-shyness-forest-canopy.

2 See Doctrine and Covenants 76:7–10; 1 Corinthians 13:12.

3 See Proverbs 9:6.

4 Meggan Watterson, Instagram, https://www.instagram.com/p/CSVXsiJMbGL/.

5 Roger Cook, *The Tree of Life: Image for the Cosmos* (New York: Thames and Hudson), 18.

6 Mircea Eliade, *Myth of the Eternal Return* (Princeton, NJ: Princeton University Press), 17–18.

7 Jacob 4:13.

8 Barker, "Wisdom and the Stewardship of Knowledge," 4.

9 Mosiah 8:20.

10 Barker, "Where Shall Wisdom Be Found?" 2.

11 Book of Wisdom (or Wisdom of Solomon) 8:12–20 (New Revised Standard Version), https://biblia.com/books/nrsv/Wis6.12.

12 James 1:5 (NIV).

13 "Gaze on the raz nihyeh (the mystery of becoming) and know the paths of everything that lives." Qumran Texts, 4Q418 fr. 43.

14 Ben Sira 24:15.

15 Exodus 30:23–25.

16 Barker, "Where Shall Wisdom Be Found?" 8.

17 Barker, "Where Shall Wisdom Be Found?" 1.

18 32 Clementine Recognitions 1.45–6, translation in Ante Nicene Fathers, vol. 8, accessed July 15, 2021, https://oll.libertyfund.org/title/coxe-ante-nicene-fathers-volume-8.

19 32 Clementine Recognitions 1.45–6, translation in Ante Nicene Fathers, vol. 8.

20 2 Corinthians 2:14, 16.

21 Cynthia Bourgeault, "Introducing the Imaginal," November 13, 2018, https://cynthiabourgeault.org/2018/11/13/introducing-the-imaginal/.

22 Cook, *Tree of Life*, 8.

23 Cook, *Tree of Life*, 9.

24 Cook, *Tree of Life*, 9.

25 Jorie Graham, "Jorie Graham: Runaway," *Between the Covers Podcast*, April 1, 2021, https://tinhouse.com/podcast/jorie-graham-runaway/.

26 See Alma 32.

27 Alma 32:27.

28 1 Thessalonians 5:17, 18.

29 Alma 32:33.

30 Alma 32:42.

31 Neal A. Maxwell, "Why Not Now?" *Ensign*, November 1974.

32 Karen L. King, *The Gospel of Mary Magdala: Jesus and the First Woman Apostle* (Santa Rosa, CA: Polebridge Press, 2003), 71.

33 Jehanne de Quillan, *The Gospel of the Beloved Companion: The Complete Gospel of Mary Magdalene* (Foix, France: Éditions Athara, 2010), 80.

34 King, *Gospel of Mary Magdala*, 80.

35 Bruce R. McConkie, *The Mortal Messiah: From Bethlehem to Calvary* (Salt Lake City: Deseret Book, 1979–81), 2:205–6.

36 Luke 17:21.

37 Richard Rohr, Richard Rohr's Daily Meditation, Center for Action and Contemplation, May 11, 2021, https://cac.org/the-great-love-song-2021-05-11/.

38 Doctrine and Covenants 38:2.

39 Acts 2:17.

40 Ross Gay, *The Book of Delights: Essays* (Chapel Hill, NC: Algonquin Books of Chapel Hill, 2019), 50.

41 hooks, *All About Love*, 93.

42 From "In Memoriam A. H. H."

43 Richard L. Rubenstein, *After Auschwitz: History, Theology, and Contemporary Judaism* (Baltimore: Johns Hopkins University Press, 1992), 302.

44 The image of a serpent wrapped around a staff is the universal medical symbol.

45 2 Timothy 3:7.

46 Japanese *in-yō*. In Eastern thought, yin and yang are the two complementary forces that make up all aspects and phenomena of life. "Yin is a symbol of earth, femaleness, darkness, passivity, and absorption. It is present in even numbers, in valleys and streams, and is represented by the tiger, the color orange, and a broken line. Yang is conceived of as heaven, maleness, light, activity, and penetration. It is present in odd numbers, in mountains, and is represented by the dragon, the colour azure, and an unbroken line. The two are both said to proceed from the Great Ultimate, their interplay on one another (as one increases the other decreases) being a description of the actual process of the universe and all that is in it. In harmony, the two are depicted as the light and dark halves of a circle." *Encyclopedia Britannica*, s.v. "yinyang," accessed April 5, 2021, https://www.britannica.com/topic/yinyang.

47 Walt Whitman, "Song of Myself, 51," https://poets.org/poem/song-myself-51.

48 Chieko N. Okazaki, "Grace and Glory: Strength from Our Savior," in *Women in the Covenant of Grace: Talks Selected from the 1993 Women's Conference Sponsored by Brigham Young University and the Relief Society*, ed. Dawn Hall Anderson and Susette Fletcher Green (Salt Lake City: Deseret Book, 1994), 243–44.

49 1 Enoch 24:4.

50 Barker, "Where Shall Wisdom Be Found?" 5.

51 Barker, "Where Shall Wisdom Be Found?" 5.

52 2 Enoch 8:4.

53 Barker, "Where Shall Wisdom Be Found?" 7.

54 Barker, "Where Shall Wisdom Be Found?" 7.

55 See Revelation 2:7; 22:14.

56 Barker, "Where Shall Wisdom Be Found?" 7.

57 Proverbs 3:18 (NIV).

58 Kathryn Knight Sonntag, "Cube of Fire," in *The Tree at the Center* (Evansville, IN: By Common Consent, 2019), 62. Reprinted with permission from BCC Press.